WEST AFRICAN FOLKTALES

STEVEN H. GALE

NTC Publishing Group
Lincolnwood, Illinois USA

Cover design: Ophelia Chambliss
Cover illustration: Paula Weber
Interior illustrations: Risa Kleban

To the memories of my mother, Mary Wilder Hasse,
and my brother, Bill;
to Kathy, Shannon, Ashley, Kristin, and my father, Norman A. Gale,
and Linda;
and to the Goodwins and the Johnsons;
as always,
with all my love and thanks.

Contents

Liberia

Mali

Nigeria

Senegal

Acknowledgments

$\mathcal{G}$athering these tales was a pleasure for me, largely because of the enthusiastic help provided by my students at the University of Liberia and the kindness with which I was treated by all of the Liberians whom I met during my stay in their country. I thank them for this. I hope they will be pleased that their tales will now be shared with people from other countries and cultures.

I also appreciate the work done by my secretary, Elaine Wesley, in checking sources and all of the other important details that go into producing a manuscript. Reference librarian Karen Pope, formerly of Kentucky State University's Blazer Library, was helpful in securing reference materials for me. In addition, I want to acknowledge the kindness of Professor Gilbert Doho (University of Yaoundé), who introduced me to sources for tales from Cameroon, and Professor Michael Unuakhalu (Kentucky State University, formerly of Nigeria), who assisted me by reviewing the facts in my Introduction and Afterword.

As always, I want to thank my wife, Kathy, and my three daughters, Shannon, Ashley, and Kristin, for their encouragement and inspiration, and especially for their patience.

Introduction

*T*he geography of the countries that comprise West Africa varies tremendously, from savannahs to deserts to mountains to forests, from the coast of the Atlantic Ocean to the hinterlands one thousand miles inland as the crow flies. The cultures represented are just as diverse, as demonstrated by the people's attitudes toward their storytelling. For instance, while many of the tales are told in a stylized manner, with interaction between the audience and the *griot* or *gewel* (or whatever the storyteller is called in a particular culture), there are vast differences among the types of tales, the purposes of the tales, and the styles in which the tales are told. Songs are often included—indeed, some tales are delivered as ballads and are accompanied by a guitar or a drum. In some societies, such as the Burundi, the delivery has been described as being "hot," that is, noisy, blustery, full of motion, and eloquently loquacious, whereas the typical Senegambian delivery, as seen in the performances of the Wolof, is more "cool," subdued, or spare. In addition to the didactic tales that Westerners are familiar with, there are also riddle tales (used to provoke audience discussion), taunting tales (used to point out the faults of others), and tales told purely for their entertainment value (a nice example of "popular culture").

Traditionally, an important function of folktales in West Africa has been to educate, as the older generation imparts knowledge to younger members of the family, tribe, societal unit, or ethnic group both informally in everyday life and more formally within the context of the bush schools. (This educational function of folktales is common in European and Western societies in general and has been a primary function particularly since the early eighteenth century, when written versions became fairly easy to obtain and were often used as models in teaching children to read.) African tales interest and amuse audiences, while passing along historical and religious myths, lessons about preferred social behavior, and practical advice related to daily activities such as hunting, farming, childrearing, governing, and so forth. In a country such as Liberia, where in 1987 a mere 35 percent of the children attended elementary school and just 25 percent of the total population was literate, the folktale is an extremely important educational medium.

There are forty-two West African folktales in this volume. Twenty-three of the selections come from Liberia; the balance are from fourteen other countries. Besides looking for a variety of the best and most interesting tales available, I also wanted to include at least one each from as many West African countries as possible.

Exactly what "West African" means, however, is not as simple to delineate as might be expected. While the concept of place is fundamental to most Africans, as it is to most of the peoples of the world, political—that is national—boundaries that take on a special significance in the West often are of considerably less importance in Third World countries. In part this is because the inhabitants of the Third World have not customarily thought of themselves as belonging to a geographically delineated nation in the same way that Westerners do. Third World life has not lent itself to such discriminations in the past. For many, "nation" was defined as those people in the clan, or those who were culturally and genetically related, no matter where the group migrated.

Additionally, and this is particularly true over the past fifty years, political boundaries in the Third World have undergone continual change as old countries disappear, new countries come into being, and borders shift according to political whim or military fortune. Searching maps of sub-Saharan Africa in the 1990s for countries or borders that existed before the 1940s or that were in existence in the 1950s or the 1960s reveals how dramatically and how frequently the geopolitical face of Africa has been altered in this relatively short time. Change has been the constant in this part of the world.

Even some contemporary experts in the field of West African studies sometimes have trouble defining exactly which countries on the continent constitute what is called "West Africa." Generally speaking, though, the Sahara Desert is accepted as the northern boundary, obviously the Atlantic Ocean serves as the western boundary, and the Sawhills and Lake Chad are considered the eastern boundary. Cameroon—where the thousand-mile-long coastline that parallels the equator turns and begins its southern plunge—is thought of as the southernmost nation in West Africa. Interestingly, though, designations have shifted over the years, and countries on the Atlantic coast up to Mauritania and down to and including Angola (which lies about five hundred miles to the south of Cameroon) have been numbered among the West African states in the nineteenth and early part of the twentieth century. Two of these far southern nations—Gabon and Angola—are represented in this book.

Within these boundaries the following countries can be designated "West African": in the north is Senegal; moving southward on the Atlantic coast one finds Gambia, Guinea-Bissau, Guinea, Sierra Leone, Liberia, Ivory Coast (Côte d'Ivoire), Ghana, Togo, Benin, Nigeria, and in the south, Cameroon; the inland nations of Mali, Niger, and Burkina Faso might also be included under this rubric.

This collection came about as a result of several circumstances that occurred during the time that I spent in Liberia as a Fulbright Professor. From July 1973 to July 1974, I taught American and English literature courses and drama at the University of Liberia. Located in the country's capital city, Monrovia, the university had an enrollment of approximately 1,700 students, most of whom were from "up-country" (that is, from anywhere outside Monrovia). In addition to teaching, I directed the University Players in several plays, two of which were based to some degree on local folkloric traditions. In preparing for the performances I had numerous discussions with cast members about the presentation of the religious and mythical elements in the plays. I later taught an American literature survey course that included selections from Mark Twain's *Huckleberry Finn* and Herman Melville's *Moby Dick* among the reading assignments. Some of the actors from the University Players were taking this course, and when the discussion again centered on the religious and mythical aspects of the work, the class became excited by certain parallels. They decided to bring in specimen folktales from their own tribes that dealt with the same themes as those found in the readings (relationships between humankind and nature and between humans and god, the use of magic and prophecy, and so forth). The individual tales were translated for the class by the tellers and a general discussion followed.

Although the concepts of studying folktales and the differences between oral and printed texts were new to the students, they responded enthusiastically and showed good insight into the nature of the stories that they were examining. It should be noted that the "database" involved primarily Liberian tales,[1] some of which were told or recollected under what might be considered artificial circumstances (including an absence of notations regarding the oral performance elements) and were interpreted by university students. Based on the sources available to them from their tribal recollections and the material presented in class, the students arrived at a number of conclusions.

First, the language used by the storytellers is the vernacular, the everyday language of the speaker as opposed to the language associated with education. This does not mean that the raconteur, the tale-teller, was uneducated, merely that the level of usage was not that of the university.

Second, the class categorized the tales according to the type of characters involved: human or animal. In those stories featuring animal characters, the animals represent human characteristics and the same animals are extratribal, appearing throughout Liberia and usually with the same anthropomorphic attributes. There is a whole series of Spider-and-Monkey tales, for example, in which Spider symbolizes greed and Monkey typifies intelligence. These Spider/Monkey parables are so popular that native teachers in up-country mission or church schools often use them to illustrate points in the

1. Reflecting the background of the Americo-Liberian community of Monrovia, one of the folktales discussed by the class could be traced back to settlers who brought the tale with them from their former home on the island of Grenada in the West Indies. People also have emigrated to Liberia from countries other than the United States and the Caribbean, naturally, and another story was brought by a student's grandparents when they traveled to Liberia from Nigeria.

classroom.[2] Animal stories are typically anecdotal in nature and usually include trickery of some sort.[3] At times there is even double trickery, with the resolution of the tale depending on the trickster being tricked in the end.

Third, the subject matter tends to fit into five loose classifications. The stories are concerned with: (a) greed; (b) pride; (c) a lack of faith (sometimes seen as representative of a humans-versus-nature theme); (d) untrustworthiness; and (e) historical narratives used to explain why things are done in certain ways, how specific habits or practices evolved, or how a precise location has taken on a sacred significance.

It should be mentioned that this classification scheme may embody a slightly distorted picture of the average topics presented in Liberian folktales. The stories recorded by the class are, for the most part, tales told openly throughout a village—by a grandparent, a friend, or a schoolteacher. In order to give a completely accurate representation it would be necessary to include examples of narratives told only among the memberships of the religious societies which form the substructure of the tribal groups, primarily the Poro (male) and Sande (female), and those associated by their totem animals (such as the snake or leopard). It would also be worthwhile to trace the dissemination of biblical tales introduced by Christian missionaries and tales from the Koran carried by the itinerant Muslim traders (known as "Charlies") who speak Pidgin English, Mandingo, or a variant of Swahili.

Fourth, there are common stylistic characteristics that have evolved in the oral tradition. The openings are fairly conventional, estab-

---

2. Such usage is recorded by anthropologists John Gay and Michael Cole in *The New Mathematics and an Old Culture: A Study of Learning among the Kpelle of Liberia* (New York, 1967).

3. In addition to Liberia, in places as far apart as Sierra Leone, Ghana, and Benin, Spider is frequently the trickster character and is known by the name Anansi. In fact, the popularity of this character is such that it appears under various names in the folklore of cultures throughout West Africa. Known as Gizo Kwaki Nancy in some areas, Spider's fame has spread even to the New World, where West Indians still refer to the character as Anansi and the Gullah in South Carolina call it Aunt Nancy.

lishing setting and characters. Often, however, there is relatively little descriptive material or local detail supplied, probably because it is assumed that the audience is familiar with the area in which the story is set.

The storytellers are usually garrulous, and audiences apparently prefer lengthy accounts. The sounds being spoken are almost as important as what is being said (as evidenced in the translations where some words or phrases are occasionally inserted simply as tags and have no real meaning[4]). As Esther Warner, the author of several books about Liberia, observed, "The whole art of African storytelling lies in taking a tale familiar to all and working on it in one's imagination until one can bring every act and emotion to life in the audience." Liberians truly enjoy orators whose "words fill the mouth like rice fills the belly."

Several other characteristics are possibly related to the Liberian appreciation for wordiness. At times the fables include arbitrary or inexplicable actions; very few provide an explicit, spoken moral at their conclusion; many end abruptly. Again, these traits may be indicative of the Liberian ranking of form over content. Since the majority of the listeners would already know most of the accounts being recited, they would be more impressed by *how* the tale is told than by *what* it says.

There have been many scholarly examinations of the characteristics of folktales (collectors and editors such as Roger D. Abrahams, Harold Courlander, Richard M. Dorson, and Paul Radin among them), so there is no need to repeat their detailed findings here. From a literary standpoint, though, it can be said that these tales have certain characteristics in common. All of them are told in the third person voice, the language is informal vernacular, and the narrative structure is simple and straightforward. At the same time, Western audiences may find a perceived lack of logic in the tales unsettling, for the stories are not structured according to the logic

---

4. The scholarly term for these tags is "ideophones"; they are a common component in the oral style employed by raconteurs.

of short stories, television programs, or movies. Folktales are a completely different genre and medium, and the expectations of both the tellers and the hearers are unlike those that inform the Western literary tradition. Why, for instance, are a magic pea *and* a magic word needed to open a hidden cave in a mountain (as in "Stealing from Thieves")? Because the teller enjoys adding a little twist in the telling and the listener appreciates the effort.

Typically, there is a tension between good and bad, occasionally involving overt religious elements. This antagonism is frequently couched in terms of a conflict between honesty and trickery. Additionally, commonplace cultural elements are regularly included. Proverbs may be interwoven into the tales as well. The tales include dialogue, and although the characters are largely undefined they are not stereotypes *per se*. Anthropomorphism is present, as is symbolism, but there is not always an abundance of other common literary devices such as imagery and metaphors.

All of the translations of the tales into English were done by the individual class members, who represented a cross-section of Liberia's major tribal units. English, the one common language spoken throughout Liberia, is taught nationwide and is the official national language, though this has been under debate and either Kpelle or Bassa may be adopted in its place.

In editing and retelling these tales I have translated them into standard English. That is, I have corrected obvious misspellings and punctuation, usage, vocabulary, and grammatical errors. While I have tried to preserve as much of the original as possible, sometimes it was necessary to reword passages for clarity—but I have tried to do so in a manner that retains the flavor of the original.

Finally, just as a play is not wholly a play until it is performed, folktales are a form of performance art and they are not fully realized until they, too, are being told to a live audience. It is only then that the unique style of each storyteller's oral presentation is evident. Unfortunately, the one component that cannot be reproduced on the printed page is the element of performance, which embodies multiple and complex nonverbal behaviors and meanings. As a result, the literary aspects of the tales included in this anthology are foregrounded, but it is hoped that the essence of the tales has been captured and transmitted in these published versions.

West African Folktales was not meant to be primarily a scholarly study. Instead, my intent is to provide an opportunity for readers to be exposed in an enjoyable way to the folktales of West Africa and through these tales come to learn something about the West African peoples and their cultures. Those readers who want more information on the backgrounds of these tales and the history of this region might turn to the Afterword on page 197.

The Bushbuck and the Leopard

ANGOLA

*A*ngola, which was still a Portuguese colony as late as the early twentieth century, is the home of the Ovimbundu, speakers of the Umbundu language. In this Angolan tale the speaker uses animal characters to impart knowledge that would be useful for his human audience. The bushbuck, duiker, and klipspringer are varieties of African antelopes.

The Bushbuck and the Leopard

*A*mong the animals who lived in the heavily forested ravine called a *kloof* were the Leopard and the Bushbuck. Because he was by nature a meat eater, Leopard wished to eat Bushbuck. Every day Leopard would wait in the bushes beside a stream hoping to pounce on Bushbuck when Bushbuck came for a drink. However, when Bushbuck visited the stream he hopped like a duiker and he jumped about like a klipspringer, bounding from side to side along the path. Whether coming to the water or returning to his home, Bushbuck always followed this practice.

Leopard became hungrier and hungrier. Finally, unable to catch Bushbuck because his prey could bound from one side of the narrow ravine to the other, and knowing that no one was likely to bring him anything to eat, Leopard decided, "Haka![1] I will go elsewhere to hunt for my food."

For many years Leopard tried to follow Bushbuck's spoor[2] in order to catch him between his lair and the stream. Whenever Leopard got to the *kloof,* though, he lost Bushbuck's smell because Bushbuck bounded from side to side so much. By the time that Leopard gave up his search for Bushbuck, Bushbuck was already home safely in his bed and Leopard never did catch him. Ultimately, Bushbuck became very old and died of natural causes.

The lesson that we can learn from this story, say the elders, is that "Bushbuck does not try to kill Leopard with his horns; he uses his wits to stay alive."

---

1. *Haka,* a common exclamation used by the Ovimbundu to indicate emotions such as frustration, anger, or surprise.
2. *Spoor* means the odor, track, or trail of an animal.

Stealing from Thieves

In Benin they tell the story "Stealing from Thieves," which is a recounting of how Joseph became a wealthy man. It is similar to the story "Ali Baba and the Forty Thieves" from A Thousand and One Nights.

Stealing from Thieves

*M*any years ago six very successful thieves made their home in a mountain. In this mountain they kept all of the gold that they had stolen, in sacks piled very high.

In a town not far from the village there lived two young brothers, Jean and Joseph. When they came of the age to earn their own living, the two brothers decided to try their hand at selling wood. Each morning they would go into the forest to cut down trees that they would then chop up into firewood and sell at the marketplace for one franc a bundle. Invariably, Jean spent most of his money as quickly as he earned it. Joseph, however, saved most of the money that he earned. The two brothers lived in this manner for some time.

Then one morning, while Joseph was in the forest taking a break from cutting the firewood, he decided to climb a large tree to see what he could see. Nearby was the mountain where the thieves lived. Joseph was fascinated by the mountain because he could see that all of the brush and trees had been removed from it. He decided to stay in the tree until he could find out why it had been cleared.

Normally, the thieves went out to go about their business early in the morning and returned in the afternoon. Joseph had not been waiting in the tree for long when the six thieves returned to their mountain home.

Since the mountain was an enchanted mountain, the thieves needed magic to open it up so that they could get into their home. The secret to the thieves' obtaining entrance into their mountain stronghold was a magical pea. The paramount thief took the pea out of a pouch, which had been hidden under a rock on the side of the mountain, and placed it on the ground. He then pushed the pea into the earth with his foot and said, "Open." At this the mountain opened and the thieves entered.

From his perch high in the tree, Joseph could look inside the mountain when the door opened. What he saw amazed him. The mountain was full of sacks of gold and the many fine things that the thieves had stolen. Early the next morning, Joseph hurried back to the forest. He again climbed the tree and watched for the thieves. Soon they came out of the mountain and prepared to go off to do their business. Before they left, the chief again took the pea out of the pouch, placed it on the ground, and pushed it into the earth with his foot. This time he said, "Close," and the mountain closed.

Joseph waited in the tree all day and, sure enough, that afternoon the thieves returned and the whole process was repeated. Joseph went home that night so excited that he could hardly sleep. The following morning he returned to the tree, and again the thieves left and returned as they had previously. Now this time Joseph, who was an educated man and could read and write, had brought along a piece of paper and a pencil. He very carefully wrote down exactly what the thieves did to open and close the mountain, and he even sketched a detailed map of where the pea was to be found and what was said.

The next day when the thieves left to go about their business, Joseph was once more watching from his tree. No sooner was the gang out of sight than Joseph was off, down the tree and up the mountainside. As soon as he reached the mountain, Joseph went to the secret rock where the pouch with the magical pea was hidden. He took the pea out of the pouch, placed it on the ground, and pushed it into the earth with his foot. Then he said to the mountain, "Open." Just as he had commanded, the mountain opened. Joseph quickly went to work picking up bags of gold and carrying them outside, where he hid them in the forest. He was no longer interested in earning his living by cutting firewood.

Soon Joseph had so much gold that he could not hide it any longer. He went to the king and asked for enough property so that he could build a great compound. The king gladly provided Joseph with the land, and Joseph hired many workmen to come to build a house for him. Each day while the workmen were building the house, Joseph disappeared into the forest. When he came back late in the afternoon, he always brought with him more bags of gold. As the number of bags of gold grew, so did the house grow in size. Before many days the house was several stories high. In fact, it was taller even than the king's palace.

By now Joseph was well respected among the villagers because of his great wealth, and he married the most beautiful girl in the village.

Joseph's brother, Jean, was still very poor. He continued to eke out a living by searching the forest for firewood, but he also continued to spend the money that he earned as quickly as it was placed in his hand. One day he decided to visit his brother. Joseph greeted Jean happily and invited him to share a meal. After the brothers had finished eating, Joseph offered Jean a sack full of money.

Jean did not want to take the money. "I am not interested in taking your money," he said. "I only want to know how you became so wealthy. After all," Jean said, "we used to go into the forest together to gather firewood, and you have become rich but I am still poor. All I ask, my brother, is that you tell me how to become rich too. If you don't, I will have to kill you." With that Jean took out a knife and threatened his brother.

Joseph looked at him. "If I tell you, you will only be killed yourself."

"Why do you say I will be killed?"

"If you try to do what I have done," replied Joseph, "you will almost certainly die. You will not be able to do the things that I have done."

"Don't worry about me, my brother, If you tell me what you did, I will be able to do it even better."

Joseph explained what had happened when he climbed the tree, and he even took Jean into the forest and showed him the exact tree to climb. Then he went home. No sooner did Jean climb to the top of the tree than the thieves returned to their mountain home. As they did when Joseph had watched them previously, the thieves removed the magical pea from its hiding place and proceeded with their ritual. When the chief said the word, "Open," the mountain opened for them.

Jean was so intent on becoming rich that he did not even go home that night. He spent the whole time in the tree. Then the next morning, when the thieves went off to do their business, he scurried down the tree and up the mountain and followed the magical ritual to cause the mountain to open. As had his brother, Jean gathered sacks of gold. When he was ready to leave, though, in his excitement he forgot what to say. He could not remember the word "Open." The only word that he could think of in his panic was "Close." So, instead of commanding the mountain to open, he demanded that it remain closed. Thus, when the thieves returned in the afternoon, they had difficulty getting the mountain to open for them, since Jean had ordered it to stay sealed.

One of the thieves guessed that there must be a man inside their mountain for it to be behaving so strangely. Finally, after a great struggle, the thieves managed to open the mountain by brute force. Once inside they looked for the man, and it was not long before they found Jean sitting on the sacks of gold that he had intended to take with him.

"What are you doing here?" they asked him.

"I am doing what my brother Joseph did," answered Jean. "He came here before me and took away many sacks of gold. That is how he became so rich, and he told me how I could become rich too."

"Is that the Joseph who lives in the house that is bigger than the king's house?"

"Yes," said Jean.

On learning what had become of their money, the thieves became so angry that they killed Jean. Then they cut him apart and nailed the pieces of his body to the side of the mountain.

The next day Joseph came looking for his brother, whom he had not seen for two days. He found the pieces of his brother's body nailed to the mountain. These he took down and put inside his sack and returned home with it.

When he got home, Joseph asked all of the leather workers of the village to come to his home. "Who is the best stitcher of you all?" he asked. "If I were to kill a goat and cut it into pieces, who could sew it back together again?" The oldest leather worker there, a man of great skill, said that he thought that he could do such a job. Joseph sent for a goat, which they killed and cut into many pieces. The old man sewed it back together.

Joseph asked the ancient leather worker to return that night. When the man did so, Joseph brought out the sack with the pieces of his brother's body in it. The old man sewed the pieces together, and he and Joseph buried Jean.

When the thieves returned after Joseph had taken his brother's body, naturally the pieces of Jean's body were no longer nailed to the mountain. The thieves discussed the matter for some time. Finally, they concluded that it must have been Joseph, a brave man, who had found Jean's body and had buried it. Beside themselves with anger, they now began to plot to kill Joseph. The following day they sent one of their members to the village to talk to the leather workers to find out who could sew the best of them all. When the old leather worker identified himself, the thief questioned him and confirmed that indeed it was Joseph who had retrieved his brother's body and buried it. When the thief returned to the mountain and told his comrades what he had learned, they sent out a call for all of the thieves in the neighborhood to come together. In the meantime, another of the six thieves went to Joseph's house on the pretext of selling him many sacks of salt. "I will be able to bring these sacks to you about midnight," he told Joseph.

That evening, Joseph went for a walk but his wife stayed behind to work in the cassava patch. While Joseph was gone, the thieves arrived with many empty sacks. They went into the house and all of the thieves but the pretend salt seller climbed into the sacks. He said to them, "When I return at midnight, I will whistle for you. All of you climb out of your sacks quickly and come to me, and we will kill and rob Joseph." The pretend salt seller then closed the sacks. Fortunately, Joseph's wife had looked through the window and seen what they were doing.

When Joseph returned home, his wife told him what she had seen and heard. Joseph said to her, "We must prepare a charm against these thieves." Together the two of them made a magical potion out of water and special herbs they had gotten from a witch doctor. The potion was so strong that if one drop of it touched a person, he would die immediately. Joseph then placed three stools at the table. He also took a pistol and gave one to his wife as well. "My wife, I am going to invite the thief to dinner. If I touch my foot with yours, that will be a signal to shoot him." He then sent a boy to invite the thief to eat.

When the thief arrived, he said, "I cannot eat with you. My sacks of salt are below and I am afraid in these perilous times that someone might steal them." Joseph touched his wife's foot with his own, and the couple both pulled out their pistols and shot the thief dead.

Below, the thieves in the sacks heard the shots. "What is that shooting?" they wondered. "Perhaps Joseph is killing some meat for his dinner," guessed one of them.

Now, Joseph went downstairs with the poisonous potion. Pretending to be the thief who he had just killed, he went to each sack and said to the men in it, "Here is some medicine. It will make you strong for when we kill Joseph." He gave some of the potion to the men in the first sack, and the sack fell to the ground. Joseph continued going from sack to sack doing the same thing and each time the sack fell to the ground, the men inside it dead.

The next morning Joseph went to the king and told him all that had happened. The king could hardly believe such a wondrous tale, but Joseph took him to the house and showed him the sacks with the dead thieves in them. The king was so delighted that Joseph had rid the country of so many thieves that he had a road built to the mountain, and he decreed that all of the gold that was there would be Joseph's.

The Chief's Daughter

*A*mong the Gurensi people of
*Burkina Faso (formerly Upper Volta), the parable of "The
Chief's Daughter" is told to explain a common pursuit
among peoples of many cultures.*

The Chief's Daughter

*M*any years ago the chief of the Gurensi tribe learned that he had to make a long journey for diplomatic reasons. He had a beautiful young daughter, and he was worried about her being taken care of while he was gone. After much thought, he called his friend Money to him. "My friend," said the chief, "I must go on a long journey. I will be gone for one or two months, or perhaps even longer. I do not know how long I will be away. While I am gone, I ask that you take care of my daughter. If any suitors come seeking her hand during that time, you are to tell them to go away until I return."

"My chief," replied Money, "I will be happy to do as you bid. You have no need to fear for your daughter's welfare."

So the chief bade farewell to his daughter and left to travel far away. One month passed, and he did not return. A second month passed, and still he did not return. Several more months passed, and the chief did not return. In the meantime, young men began coming to inquire about the possibility of obtaining the chief's daughter's hand in marriage. Each time one of these young men appeared, Money turned him away. Still, after the chief had been gone for many months, Money began to worry. "I wonder if something has happened to the chief," he thought. "Perhaps he is not going to return."

Then one day another young suitor came seeking marriage with the chief's daughter. When he asked for permission to marry her, Money said to him, "If you want to marry the girl, you must make the arrangements with me, for the chief has been gone for a long time. I do not think that he is going to return, and her welfare is my responsibility."

For some time the eager suitor and Money argued about the marriage settlement. Finally, they decided that the young man would pay many bags of cowrie shells,[1] bolts of bright cloth, some heavy copper bars, and even a horse. Once this bride price had been determined, it did not take the young man long to gather together the items of the marriage settlement to exchange for the chief's daughter's hand. As soon as he had collected all of the goods, he gave them to Money and took the girl far away to his village. Money was very pleased with himself because of this transaction, for he had become very rich as a result of it.

Then one day news came that the chief was on his way home. Money became distraught. "My friend, the chief, put me in charge of his daughter's affairs. He instructed me not to listen to the wooing of her suitors. Now I have permitted her marriage and I have taken a marriage settlement. Even though I thought that he was dead, how can I face him when he returns?"

Money quickly packed up his family and all of his belongings and set out to travel as far away from the village as he could go.

When the chief arrived at his home, the first thing that he asked was, "Where is my daughter?"

The people of the village explained what had happened: "Money arranged for a bride price with a suitor, and your daughter has been married and taken away."

The chief was furious. "Bring Money to me," he shouted angrily. "We are sorry," the people said, "but we do not know where he is. He has fled out of the country."

The chief grew more furious. He demanded that the villagers find Money, no matter where he had gone, and bring him back to the

1. Traditionally, cowrie shells have been used throughout West Africa as money. They are also used as decorations on masks, carvings, houses, and a variety of other objects. Occasionally, they are even found in inlaid designs on the walls of important buildings.

village. The villagers were bewildered. They did not know where to look. The chief raged. "Look everywhere. You must continue looking until you have found Money."

Years and years passed as the people looked for Money. They could not find him anywhere. They traveled far and wide looking for the chief's old friend and asking everybody whom they met whether they knew where Money was. After some time the chief died. Even so, his people continued to look for Money. In fact, that is why people still are seeking Money everywhere today.

The Pitcher

*T*he *orphan is a popular subject in West African folklore. From the Cameroon comes "The Pitcher," in which Koffi, an orphan boy, must replace his stepmother's pitcher, which he has just broken. According to the storyteller, this story is meant to explain why orphans are well-treated—presumably because if the stepmother had treated Koffi well, she would not have brought misfortune on herself and her natural son.*

The Pitcher

*W*hen Koffi's mother died at his birth, the boy became the ward of a stepmother. She was a wicked, mean stepmother, and she gave Koffi many menial tasks to perform as he grew up. One of these tasks was to fetch the water.

One morning, coming back from filling the pitcher with water, Koffi stumbled, and the pitcher broke into a myriad of shards. The boy could only stand and look at the remains of what had once been a fine pitcher. Soon, his stepmother appeared. "Yah! My pitcher," she cried. "You've broken my favorite pitcher. *You've broken my only pitcher!*" Koffi stood silently. The stepmother shouted at him, "You must replace my pitcher. You must find one exactly like the one that you have broken. Go, and don't come back until you have it."

Koffi turned and began his long journey in search of a suitable pitcher. The longer he walked, the better he felt. At home his stepmother had made life miserable for him with her insults and punishments. Now he met friendly people who were happy to talk with him and animals with whom he joked.

One day Koffi came to the bank of a very large river. In this water there lived a crocodile as big as a mountain.

The huge crocodile opened a mouth with sharp teeth as large as trees and said, "How did you come to my house, child? From the beginning of the world no man has ever visited this country. How would you like to be eaten?"

"Please, sir, I am a poor orphan. Please do not eat me."

The crocodile moved closer.

"Well, if you are determined to eat me, let me tell you my story first," said the boy.

Koffi told the enormous reptile the sad story of his life from his birth and his mother's death up to the point where he was confronting the beast because of the stepmother's broken pitcher. The crocodile was so touched that he shed real tears, not just crocodile tears. "I'll tell you what," said the crocodile. "It is difficult for me to scrub my back. If you do that for me, I will reward you by letting you see your mother and by helping you get a pitcher exactly like the one that you broke."

Immediately, Koffi agreed to undertake this daunting task. He picked up a brush and sponge that the crocodile had been using to bathe himself, and he began the long, laborious task of washing the crocodile's back. When the job was done satisfactorily, the crocodile said to Koffi, "Stay on my back and we will start our journey to your mother and the pitcher." The crocodile began swimming out to the middle of the river.

After several days, the travelers arrived in front of a tiny, dirty door. The crocodile said, "Knock on the door."

As soon as Koffi knocked, the door opened with a horrific thundering sound and a gigantic creature emerged, a creature so large that its feet were in the water and its head was in the clouds. The odor of the creature was an overwhelming stench.

"What do you want, child? How did you get here?" came the loud, rumbling voice of the monster.

The moment that the creature had appeared, the crocodile had disappeared, leaving Koffi alone. The orphan was more frightened than when he had confronted his stepmother or the crocodile. He was too scared to speak.

"What do you want?" repeated the monster in a voice of thunder.

As he had done with the crocodile, Koffi explained the sequence of events that led him before the monster, from his birth to that very moment.

"If your wishes are to come true, you must comb my hair," roared the gigantic creature.

As before, Koffi turned to the task. When he had finished his Herculean effort, the monster told him to turn around. When Koffi looked behind himself, he beheld a devil more horrifying than the crocodile and the monster together. And, in a voice more terrifying than that of the crocodile and the monster together, the devil screamed, "Who are you, child? What do you want?"

One more time, Koffi told the story of his travels from the moment of his birth onward, including the death of his mother, the breaking of the stepmother's pitcher, and the meetings with the crocodile and the monster. Silently, the devil led him to a place of complete darkness. After a long walk they emerged at the top of the highest mountain. The devil asked Koffi, "What did you see in the dark place?"

"I saw nothing," Koffi replied.

"If your desires are to be fulfilled, you must jump off of this mountain," the devil decreed. The mountain was so high that nothing else could be seen. There was only rock—no trees, no valley below, not even any sound to be heard.

Koffi jumped. When he landed at the bottom of the mountain, the devil was waiting for him there with two keys in its grasp. It handed him the keys and said, "Continue. You will find two doors, one on the side of the hand with which you eat, and the second on the other side. Go through the door on the side of the hand with which you eat. Under no circumstances should you even touch the door on the other side."

Koffi thanked the devil and continued his journey. When he opened the door on the side of his hand with which he ate, he found that it led to a village of old women. "Who are you, child? What do you want?" they said.

Koffi repeated his story. In fact, he repeated it to every single old woman in the village.

The oldest of the women, a gray, haggard crone, approached him. "So you want to see your mother and to find a pitcher just like the one you broke?"

"Yes."

The old women crowded around Koffi and the oldest one said to him, "If you are to achieve your goal, you must comb our hair, clean our fingernails and toenails, fetch clean water, and wash and dress each and every one of us."

One more time Koffi turned to an onerous labor. When he was finished, the oldest of the women gave him two gourds and told him how to use them. At a certain spot he was to throw one gourd to the ground. He would then be told what to do with the other.

Koffi reached the special spot after a short walk. He threw the first gourd to the ground. The moment that it landed, Koffi's mother appeared and asked him to give her the other gourd and the second key. When he did so, she handed him three more gourds. "Take this first gourd," she commanded, "and throw it to the ground as soon as you are out of the village. Hold tightly to the other two gourds, for they contain your fortune."

Koffi took the three gourds. Then his mother gave him a pitcher exactly like the one that he had broken.

When he reached the exit to the village, he threw the first gourd to the ground. As soon as he had done so, he found himself back in his own village. However, he had been gone for so many years and had grown so much that no one recognized him. Koffi gave his stepmother the duplicate pitcher. Then he threw the second gourd to the ground. As it burst open, huge castles began to emerge from the earth itself. There were so many of them and they were so big and beautiful and extravagant that no one could see them all in one glance. Then Koffi threw down the third gourd and from it came many people, all bearing gifts of great value and proclaiming him king.

Imagine how the stepmother felt at this sight. She became obsessed with the idea of her own son's becoming equal to or even greater than Koffi in power and wealth. This thought dwelt in her mind for many days and nights. Finally, she called her son to her. "You must go and do the things that Koffi did," she said. "We must become as rich and powerful as he."

The young man followed the trail that Koffi had followed so many years before. When he arrived at the river, he found the huge crocodile waiting.

"Who are you, child? What do you want?"

"My mother sent me to become as wealthy and powerful as Koffi."

"Koffi was very kind and helpful," said the crocodile.

"So am I."

"Wash my back."

"Wash your back? Why would I do that? All I want is for you to carry me across the river, and your back does not have to be clean for that."

"As you wish," said the crocodile.

"What will I find over there?"

"What you are looking for."

The crocodile took the stepmother's son on its back and carried him to the door that opened to reveal the creature whose feet were in the water and whose head was in the clouds.

"Comb my hair," the creature demanded.

"No, I am on my way to become as wealthy and powerful as Koffi, and I do not have time for you."

"Continue, then."

"What will I find along the way?"

"What you are looking for."

The monster led the stepmother's son to the devil's house and the devil took the young man to the top of the mountain as he had taken Koffi. When the stepmother's son refused to jump from the mountaintop, the devil carried him to the village of old women. There the women cried out to him, "Cut our hair, clean our fingernails, wash us, fetch fresh water for us, and we will help you find that which you seek."

"That will I never do," said the stepmother's son.

The oldest of the old women then handed him four gourds. "Use these," she said, "and you will see what you will see. When you throw the first gourd on the ground, you will be home in your own village again. When you break the other three gourds, you will see what you will see."

The stepmother's son threw the first gourd to the ground and as it broke he found himself in his own village where his triumphant mother was awaiting him. The stepmother seized the gourds from her son's hands. She quickly threw the first gourd to the ground with all of her might. Lions, leopards, hyenas, and many other kinds of fierce, wild beasts appeared immediately. Hoping to protect herself from being eaten alive, the stepmother threw the second gourd to the ground. The entire world seemed to be on fire as flames shot forth from the earth and the sky about the mother and her son. The wild beasts charged through the flames at the two humans. The stepmother quickly broke the third gourd on the ground. Suddenly the ground cracked open, and the stepmother and her son fell into the yawning chasm. The earth snapped closed behind them. All that was left were the beautiful castles and Koffi and the wealthy inhabitants of his kingdom.

Bete-tebi

*M*embers of the Nweh tribe in
the Southwest Province, Cameroon, tell the story of Bete-tebi,
a hunter who encounters a witch. The folktale was recorded
by Nol Alembong, a lecturer at the University of Yaoundé.

Bete-tebi

Once there lived on the outskirts of the forest a renowned hunter named Bete-tebi, his wife, and his dog. One day the hunter decided to go with his dog to the depths of the forest. Although he was not always very successful in his hunting, on this particular day he shot and killed all of the animals that he encountered. He hunted until dusk and then started for home.

He had gone just a short distance from his hunting ground when he discovered a hut that belonged to an old woman called Emenden.[1] She lived there with a dwarf named Begialamua.[2] Night was about to fall, and Emenden invited the hunter to stay the night at her hut. The hunter thought that Emenden was an ordinary woman. "Such old women are usually very kind and interesting," he thought, and he accepted her invitation. However, Emenden was a wicked witch. She welcomed Bete-tebi into her hut wholeheartedly.

After some time, Emenden asked Bete-tebi to give her a share of the meat that he had gotten from his hunting spree. When he took an antelope out of his hunting sack, Emenden shouted: "That is my goat that ran into the forest some time ago!" She also identified the dead fox that the man pulled out of his bag as her dog, the partridge as her chicken, and so on. From each of these animals the hunter gave her a leg. In addition, he gave her some meat to be used in preparing their evening meal.

When the evening meal was ready, to Bete-tebi's astonishment Begialamua was given no food. The poor little man had to feed on the bones and scraps of food that Emenden threw on the floor. This situation aroused the hunter's pity. Therefore, as he ate, he threw bones to his dog and simultaneously some good pieces of meat to Begialamua. Suspecting that the hunter was stubbornly or mistak-

---

1. *Emenden,* old mother.
2. *Begialamua,* a child who is worried.

enly going against the custom of her household by giving the dwarf meat, and to stop him from doing so, Emenden constantly asked Begialamua what he was eating. The dwarf replied, "Bones and rejected parts of *cocoyams*."[3]

There were two bamboo beds in the hut. That night Bete-tebi slept on one and Emenden on the other. Begialamua slept on the wood ash by the fireside. When Bete-tebi was about to go to bed, Emenden asked him, "How do I know when you are asleep?"

The hunter replied, "When you say 'Shhh' to my dog and it doesn't get up, you know that I am already asleep." Bete-tebi in his turn asked her, "And how do I also know you are asleep?"

The witch responded, "When you hear me snoring, then you know I am asleep."

Bete-tebi went to bed and within a few minutes he was asleep. Emenden got up quietly, took some herbs, and squeezed them across the doorway; a great mountain appeared and blocked the passage out of the hut. The dwarf awoke as she put the herbs away, so he knew where she kept them.

Emenden then put in the fire an iron rod with which she planned to kill the hunter. She constantly called out to Bete-tebi's dog, "Shhh," to see if its master was deeply asleep or not. Each time she called the dog, it got up almost immediately. In fact, she ought to have known that dogs never sleep deeply. Emenden was tired by now, and since the dog continued to wake up each time the woman made the sound "Shhh," indicating that its master was not yet asleep, the witch went back to bed. No sooner did she fall asleep than she started snoring.

Begialamua saw this and said to himself, "One good turn deserves another. Why should I allow this man who has been so kind to me

---

3. *Cocoyam,* a potato-like tuber known in some parts of the world as *taro.* In West African countries, cocoyams are an inexpensive source of protein and carbohydrates.

to be killed for no reason?" He woke the hunter and instructed him to leave as quickly as possible. The dwarf made the mountain at the door go away by squeezing on it the herbs that the old woman had used. He lit pieces of split bamboo and gave them to Bete-tebi to use in seeing his way through the forest, for it was extraordinarily dark.

After Bete-tebi's departure, the dwarf carefully took Emenden's calabash of oil and laid it down on the bed where the hunter had lain. After a long, profound sleep Emenden woke up and said, "Shhh." Since the dog was no longer there, there was no answer. The witch concluded that the hunter was fast asleep. She removed the red-hot iron rod from the fire and plunged it into the calabash of oil on the bed, thinking that it was the sleeping Bete-tebi. The rod burst the calabash open and oil started spilling out of it. Excited because she thought that she had killed Bete-tebi, Emenden ordered Begialamua to hurry and bring a big bowl for them to collect the fats oozing out of the hunter.

But before the dwarf could bring the bowl, Emenden noticed that the hunter and his dog were no longer there; what she had thought to be fat from the hunter was but oil from her own calabash. She angrily set out in pursuit of Bete-tebi. Whenever she saw the light shining from the lit bundle of bamboo sticks that Bete-tebi was holding, she would shout, "Bete-tebi-oo-oo!" and he would answer, "Woo'oo!" The witch called to him, "When you reach home, leave your door open-oo'o!"

On his journey home, whenever Bete-tebi came across a thorny tree he would touch it with the bamboo light so that particles of fire would remain glowing on it. The witch was so stupid that each time she got to one of these thorny trees, she believed that it was Bete-tebi standing still with the bundle of bamboo light in his hand. She would start fighting with the tree with all her might, thinking that she was fighting with Bete-tebi. "This man must have witchcraft," she thought. "If not, how can he suddenly become so thorny?" Thinking that the thorns of the tree were nails that Bete-tebi was using to fight her, she would cry out, "Bete-tebi, let's use just hands and not nails." Finally, when she realized that it was not Bete-tebi with whom she was fighting, she continued her chase.

When Bete-tebi got back home, he was so worn out that he immediately went to bed. Perhaps because Emenden's magical powers were so strong, the hunter left his door open. When she arrived and found the door open as she had instructed, she was so excited that she danced around the hunter's bed many times. She carried the bed, with Bete-tebi and his wife deeply asleep in it, and headed back to her own house.

A kind bird, who knew how wicked Emenden was, sang to try to awaken the poor couple. It sang with a sharp, clear tone: "Bete-tebi-oo'oo, hold a tree branch, else you are gone-oo!" but neither Bete-tebi nor his wife heard the bird's song. He was so tired that he slept soundly, and she was sleeping deeply, as women do. Then the bird shook a tree branch and dew fell on the pair in the bed. They woke up and the bird sang again, "Bete-tebi-oo'o, hold a tree branch, else you are gone-oo!" Emenden did not understand the bird's song, but Bete-tebi did. Unnoticed by the old woman, he and his wife clung to tree branches, and the witch carried an empty bed the rest of the way to her house.

When she arrived home, she kept the bed in her store, happy that the hunter and his wife were still sleeping in it. The store was locked and nobody dared open it without Emenden's permission.

For many years Emenden had belonged to the Ated, a communal group that used human flesh as meat for nourishment. In fact, a member's turn to invite this group to work on his or her farm essentially depended on whether he or she had human flesh to eat. Being sure that she had the two people in her store and intending to make her turn the greatest of all turns, the wicked Emenden summoned the group to work on her farm the following day. After work the people settled down to eat and drink. Emenden proudly sent Begialamua to bring the meat from the store. When he came back with the report that the couple were not there, the old woman could not believe it. She had locked the store on her return and it had not been opened since. Frowning at Begialamua's irresponsibility, especially in such a serious matter, and being sure that the couple was still in the store, she went to fetch them. She found only an empty bed. Since there was no meat, Emenden was eaten by the members of the Ated, according to the rules and regulations of the association.

A Hat Made of Smoke

*C*hi Wara from Mundum in
the Cameroon told this story to boys and girls during the
harvest period. It was recorded by Paul Mbangwana, a professor of English at the University of Yaoundé.

A Hat Made of Smoke

*I*n those days when people had many children there was a chief who had countless daughters. One of his daughters was so beautiful that her beauty had magical powers. She didn't seem a child of this world, at least not one born of normal human beings. Yet, we are told that the chief and her mother were her parents. Every man of marrying age in the chiefdom yearned to marry her. The chief, who used to turn her suitors away, was now aging, and he became very pragmatic about her marriage. He needed, before he died, to marry his daughter to the most suitable young man. But, to whom?

The king devised a contest. This contest required great imagination, for it consisted of making a hat with smoke. The chief felt that anyone who could make a hat with smoke would qualify to marry his daughter, this girl of moonly beauty. Many men who were interested in obtaining the princess's hand endeavored to accomplish this task.

Antelope tried to smoke up a room to collect smoke in order to weave a hat; he failed desperately. Monkey, Chimpanzee, Baboon, Hare, Elephant, and all types of men tried their luck. But they all failed. They concluded unanimously that it was a hopeless task, and they withdrew from the contest.

Then one day the news of the challenge reached Tortoise. He heard that everyone had failed. He, too, wanted to try. Before he began, though, he decided to talk to the chief first. He asked the chief, "Is it true, Royal Highness, that the chief is really willing to give his daughter's hand in marriage? But, Royal Highness, look. The chief needs to give me some time to accomplish this task."

The chief told him to take his time. The chief was interested in having a hat made only of smoke. This was his only demand.

Tortoise left and went to a waterfall, where he began dancing, screaming, and applauding the water. He sent somebody to tell the chief that if the chief gave him a container made of fresh blood, he would collect condensed smoke from the waterfall and he would weave an excellent hat with it.

The chief received this thought-provoking news. He went to the scene at the waterfall. He talked to Tortoise, who said, "Your Royal Highness knows that in order to collect smoke one needs a container made of fresh blood. Let His Royal Highness give me one. I will collect a good quantity of smoke and will weave for the chief as many hats as the chief desires. The chief has seen how many people and animals have failed in the task. Yet, it is such an easy demand that I make of the chief. Let the chief first give me what I have asked for. Your Royal Highness knows all things."

The chief, hearing this speech, was taken aback. He said that there was no such container. Tortoise replied that the chief's demand could not be met without a container made of fresh blood. He continued, "Look, Your Royal Highness. You have defaulted. The contest is flat. It has no meaning. Its meaning lies in the container we are awaiting from the chief. So, I'm anxiously waiting for the chief's daughter. The terms of the test are not completed, but it is finished. After all, who can shoot a gun without loading it?[1] Should I be the first in history to do such a thing? Am I to upset the order of things in this chiefdom?"

Reluctantly, and with a heart full of grief, the chief gave his daughter to Tortoise for marriage. After all, the chief himself was unable to fulfill the conditions necessary for the task that he had set. Thus, when all the formalities were fulfilled, Tortoise married the princess. He was the happiest of men and they were the most admired couple in the chiefdom. From that day, "No blood container, no smoke-hat" was a well-known saying applied to impossible tasks.

---

1. This is a proverb that means that every act has stages in its accomplishment. To shoot a gun requires first loading it with gunpowder or cartridges. To shoot a gun without loading it means to do the impossible thing.

A Test of Strength

*N*ear Libreville at the mouth of
the Gaboon River in Gabon, members of the Mpongwe tribe
tell the story "A Test of Strength." This tale reflects the seri-
ousness with which the tribespeople consider the question of
equality in strength, intelligence, and other powers. It would
seem that in a contest of strength between a tortoise, an elephant, and a hippopotamus, the tortoise would be the last of
the animals chosen. Nonetheless, as can be seen in this tale,
there is more than one way to win such a test.

A Test of Strength

$\mathcal{A}$t one time Leopard was the most powerful of all of the beasts, and therefore he was accorded the position of king of the animals. When he died, however, his children were too young to take his place, and Tortoise (who might have had a hand in Leopard's death) claimed to be among the most powerful of the animals.

Every day Tortoise boasted: "Elephant, Hippopotamus, and I are equal in power, so much so that we eat together at the same table."

The people went to Elephant and Hippopotamus and told them what Tortoise said. Both Elephant and Hippopotamus laughed at Tortoise's foolishness. "Do not pay any attention to him," they said, "he can only be pitied or despised for his foolish boasts."

One day Elephant and Hippopotamus came upon each other walking about in the forest. Hippopotamus asked, "Have you heard this foolish boast that Tortoise has been making, saying that he is as powerful as both of us?"

Elephant answered, "Yes, I have heard what he has said. But, I do not take it seriously. After all, I am Elephant. I am the biggest of the animals. In fact, my foot is as big as Tortoise's whole body. How foolish for him to say that he is as powerful as I! Still, I have not taken it upon myself to speak on this matter, for I have not heard Tortoise himself say these things."

Hippopotamus nodded. "I am following the same path. I shall say nothing until I hear Tortoise myself. Then, look out!"

The two large animals then went their separate ways.

Soon another animal, who had overheard Elephant and Hippopotamus talking, happened to meet Tortoise. This animal informed Tortoise of what he had heard: "They were threatening you. They said that they would do nothing until they heard you speak the words yourself. Then, you will be in trouble. In the meantime, though, they said that you were foolish and contemptuous."

"So," said Tortoise, "they think that I am foolish and contemptuous, do they?" He thought for a moment. "We shall see what we shall see."

Tortoise went to his wife and got his coat to cover his body. Then he went to the forest. There he found Elephant lying beneath a tree. Elephant's trunk was so long that he could not see the end of it. Elephant's ears were as big as a hut. Elephant's feet were, indeed, larger than Tortoise's entire body.

Nevertheless, Tortoise called out to Elephant, "*Mwera!*[1] I am here. Why don't you stand up to greet me?"

Elephant looked at Tortoise. Slowly he stood up. With great indignation he asked, "Who are you calling *Mwera,* Tortoise?"

"I am calling you *Mwera.*" Tortoise replied. "Are we not chums, Elephant?"

Elephant was growing increasingly angry. "I have been told that you are making certain boasts, Tortoise. Is it true that you have in fact made these boasts?"

"Don't get so angry." replied Tortoise. "I did address you as *Mwera,* but why should that cause you to berate me? Just because you are a huge mound of meat, and I am small, you think that you are more powerful and better than I am. Let us put this delusion of yours to a test. Tomorrow morning we shall engage in a tug-of-war contest."

"Why? I can smash you like a yam with one foot."

Tortoise smiled. "So what do you have to lose? You should at least be willing to engage in a contest."

---

1. *Mwera,* "chum." This term may be used only with an equal. If addressed to someone of superior rank, this term may incite a quarrel.

Elephant was unhappy with the situation that was presented to him, but finally he consented to the test.

"Good," said Tortoise. "And if one of us pulls the other over in the contest, he shall be considered the greater of the two. If neither proves stronger, then we are *Mwera*. Wait here while I go and find a vine for us to use."

Tortoise walked off into the forest to find a very long vine. When he came back he gave one end of it to Elephant. "This is your end. Tomorrow we will have our tug-of-war, and each of us will continue, not stopping to eat or sleep, until one or the other is triumphant or the vine breaks."

Tortoise went back into the forest. He continued walking until he came to Hippopotamus's town, where he hid the end of the vine. He then went to find Hippopotamus, who was bathing in the river. Tortoise called to him, "I am here, *Mwera!* Come ashore and talk to me."

Hippopotamus, bellowing in his anger, charged ashore. "Who do you call *Mwera?* Are you trying to pick a fight with me?"

"Who do I call *Mwera?*" replied Tortoise. "I am calling you *Mwera*. After all, we are equals. Let us put this to a test. Tomorrow morning we shall engage in a tug-of-war contest."

"Why? I can smash you like a yam with one foot."

Tortoise smiled. "So what do you have to lose? You should at least be willing to engage in a contest."

Like Elephant, Hippopotamus was unhappy with the situation that was presented to him, but finally he consented to the test.

"Good," said Tortoise. "And if one of us pulls the other over in the contest, he shall be considered the greater of the two. If neither proves stronger, then we are *Mwera*. Wait here while I go and find a vine for us to use."

Tortoise walked off into the forest to find a very long vine. When he came back, he gave one end of it to Hippopotamus. "This is your end. Tomorrow we will have our tug-of-war, and each of us will continue, not stopping to eat or sleep, until one or the other is triumphant or the vine breaks."

That evening both Elephant and Hippopotamus went into the forest to gather leaves for magic to make them even stronger than they already were. That night, both slept soundly.

The next morning Tortoise walked back into the forest to the middle of the vine, where he made a mark on the ground. He then shook the vine first toward one end and then toward the other. When Elephant saw the end of the vine shake, he grabbed it, as did Hippopotamus at the other end of the vine. As the old people say, "Orindi went back and forth";[2] Elephant and Hippopotamus pulled against each other, first Elephant moving Hippopotamus and then Hippopotamus moving Elephant. While Elephant and Hippopotamus continued to pull against one another, Tortoise smiled at his plan.

After a time the vine was stretched taut between Elephant and Hippopotamus, and Tortoise laughed to see it quiver from their exertions. Nothing else moved. Soon, Tortoise left the vine to seek his usual lunch of mushrooms. He ate and drank until his stomach could hold no more and then he went back home to sleep.

Late in the afternoon Tortoise arose to find out what was happening in the tug-of-war. When he reached the midpoint of the vine, it was still stretched taut, and it quivered from the efforts of Elephant and Hippopotamus. Occasionally one of the huge animals drew the other toward himself slightly, only to be drawn back the other way in turn. In spite of these momentary advantages, neither animal could succeed in overpowering his opponent.

---

2. This proverb refers to a fish called the *orindi,* which swims back and forth.

Finally, Tortoise became tired of the game. He pulled out a knife and cut the vine in half. At the two opposite ends Elephant and Hippopotamus fell backward with the sudden release of the tension and slammed into the ground with a great crashing noise. "Ah," said Tortoise, "that's that. Now I will visit Elephant with this end of the broken vine and tomorrow I will visit Hippopotamus with the other end."

Tortoise followed the vine to its end, where he found the sad Elephant soaking his legs in *juju* water.[3]

"*Mwera!*" exclaimed Tortoise. "What do you think now? Is it not true that we are *Mwera?*"

Elephant nodded. "Yes, Tortoise, I had no idea how strong you were. Indeed, when the vine broke, I fell so hard that I hurt my leg. We are truly equal. It seems that strength does not come from a large body alone. Your body is small, so I was contemptuous of you, but it turns out that we are equally strong."

Tortoise and Elephant sat down and ate a snack in celebration of Tortoise's great victory. After they played together as *Mwera* for a time, Tortoise went home to his town.

The next morning, he picked up the other end of the broken vine and went to Hippopotamus's town. There he found Hippopotamus looking sad and rubbing his head.

"*Mwera!*" Tortoise exclaimed. "What do you think now? Is it not true that we are *Mwera?*"

Hippopotamus nodded. "It was a great contest. For a long time I could not beat you nor could you defeat me. Indeed, when the vine broke, I fell so hard that I hurt my head. We are truly equal. It seems that strength does not come from a large body alone. Your body is small, so I was contemptuous of you, but it turns out that we are equally strong."

----

3. *Juju,* magic.

Tortoise and Hippopotamus sat down and ate a snack in celebration of Tortoise's great victory. After they played together as *Mwera* for a time, Tortoise went home to his town.

From that day on, whenever Tortoise, Elephant, Hippopotamus, and other animals of great strength meet for a palaver,[4] the three *Mwera* sit together on the highest stools, for they are truly equal.

---

4. *Palaver*, a discussion or debate.

Tiny Fereyel and
the Witch

*W*hat may at first seem to be a
disadvantage may actually turn out to be an advantage in
overcoming wickedness. This is the lesson that the Fulani
people of Gambia illustrate in their story "Tiny Fereyel and
the Witch."

Tiny Fereyel and the Witch

Long ago a witch named Debbo Engal and her ten beautiful daughters lived in a house deep in the bush. Over the years many young men traveled to this house to seek marriage with the daughters. Mysteriously, none of the young men were ever seen again.

The reason for this was that Debbo Engal cheerfully greeted all of the youths who came to visit her beautiful daughters and served them palm wine and good food. She entertained the youths until it became dark. Then she said, "Since it is night, and you do not know how to find your way back through the bush in the dark, you are welcome to stay here."

Of course, the suitors were happy to stay, and they soon went to sleep in the biggest hut in Debbo Engal's compound. Once the men were asleep, Debbo Engal crept up on them and killed them with a huge, sharp knife that she kept for that purpose. In the morning the witch ate the bodies of the young men, for she enjoyed the taste of human flesh.

In a village far away there lived a woman and her ten sons. When they heard about Debbo Engal's beautiful daughters, the sons eagerly prepared to visit them. Their mother begged them not to go, though, for she had heard of all of the other young men who had made such a visit and had never been heard of again. Still, her sons, with the boldness and assurance of youth, only laughed at her and said, "Our Mother, you have nothing to worry about. Each of us has grown to be a man, and you know that no woman can be our match, especially a woman who is the mother of ten such lovely daughters."

Thus, the brothers made their plans to travel to Debbo Engal's compound, and early one morning they set off on their journey. The brothers had barely disappeared from sight when their mother gave birth to an eleventh son. Unlike his brothers, however, this child was very small. Indeed, he was no larger than his mother's little finger. As soon as he was born, the youngster stood up and asked his mother, "Where are my brothers?"

Despite her amazement at the newborn's ability to talk and his knowledge that he had brothers, the mother answered that they had gone to visit Debbo Engal's daughters. At this news the youngest of the woman's sons became very agitated. "I must save them," he exclaimed. "They are in great danger." With that, he ran off along the trail that led to Debbo Engal's compound. Within minutes the young man saw his ten brothers in the distance. He called after them to wait for him, and the young men stopped to see who was raising such a racket. When the tiny boy reached them, the brothers could only wonder at who he was.

"I am Fereyel, your youngest brother," the child announced.

"Why, that cannot be so, for we are ten, and there are no more brothers," they responded. "You had better stop trying to trick us. Leave us alone if you know what is good for you."

"But you are in great danger, and I have come to save you," Fereyel cried.

When the brothers heard this, they became quite angry, and they began to beat the boy. Then the brothers continued on their journey to Debbo Engal's.

After they had traveled for some distance, one of the brothers discovered a fine cloth lying on the ground. "Look, my brothers, some careless person has dropped this beautiful cloth and I have found it. What a lucky journey this is going to be." With that, the young man picked up the cloth and draped it across his shoulder.

As the brothers continued on their way, the newly found cloth grew heavier and heavier. Finally, the young man asked one of his brothers to carry the cloth for him. The brother laughingly chided him for being so weak, but he accepted the cloth. The group had not traveled long before the second brother also grew weak under the heaviness of the cloth, and he asked a third brother to carry it for a while. This continued until each of the brothers had become tired from carrying the heavy cloth. When the tenth and oldest brother found that he could carry it no more, he sat down in weariness. As he did so, they all heard a tiny voice yelling at them derisively from inside the cloth, "Ha! It is I, Fereyel, your youngest brother. You have been carrying me, and that is why the cloth is so heavy." The ten brothers were taken aback momentarily, but soon their amazement turned to anger and they shook the cloth until Fereyel fell out of it. Once again they beat him and continued on their journey.

The brothers had not traveled much farther before one of them stepped on something. "My goodness," he shouted to his brothers, "some careless person has lost this silver ring." He placed the ring on his finger and the group once more started down the path that led to the ten beautiful maidens.

They had not gone far when the brother who had found the silver ring realized that it had grown so heavy that he could no longer lift his hand. As had happened with the lovely cloth, he passed the ring to another brother, who in turn passed it along and so on until each of the ten had become exhausted from wearing the ring. The eldest brother took the ring off to examine it, wanting to find out why it had become so heavy. Once again the tiny voice shouted out, "Why, didn't you guess? The ring is so heavy because I, Fereyel, am inside it."

The brothers quickly jumped up and surrounded the ring. They were so mad this time that they were ready to beat Fereyel with sticks. The oldest brother stopped them. "Wait," he said. "This Fereyel seems determined to come with us, and perhaps if we just let him follow along, he will not bother us anymore." The nine brothers agreed, and they set out for Debbo Engal's with the tiny Fereyel trailing behind them.

When they reached the witch's house, she hurried out to welcome them, as she had all of the previous suitors. The brothers were almost overpowered by the beauty of the ten daughters, and the young men gladly accepted Debbo Engal's invitation to savor her palm wine and fine food.

Fereyel was so small that the witch had not seen him as he stood behind his eldest brother's foot, but when the brothers went to the largest hut in the compound for their refreshments, the witch spied him. She was so amused at seeing someone so small that she asked him to join her in her own hut.

When darkness fell that evening, the wicked witch had no trouble convincing the ten brothers to spend the night, exactly as she had done with all of the suitors who had come before them. Debbo Engal then went back to her own hut and prepared a mat for Fereyel to sleep upon.

Fereyel lay down and pretended to go to sleep. Soon the witch got up and went to fetch her huge, sharp knife from where she hid it. As she did so, Fereyel said, "What are you doing?"

"Ah, my little man, I'm sorry I awakened you. I was merely trying to see if we had provisions for a good breakfast in the morning. Lie down and go to sleep." So saying, the witch lay back down and both she and Fereyel pretended to go to sleep. Some time later, Debbo Engal got up again and quietly walked to where she had hidden her huge, sharp knife.

"What are you doing?" Fereyel asked again. And, again, the witch pretended that she had just been checking on something and she lay back down. After some time the witch actually did go to sleep, which Fereyel could tell from the sound of her steady breathing. He got up silently and went out into the compound. He located the largest hut and quietly crept inside. Being careful to make no noise, as swiftly as possible he took the white gowns that his brothers wore and exchanged them with the blue robes that the witch's ten beautiful daughters wore. As quickly and quietly as he had come, he returned to Debbo Engal's hut.

No sooner had Fereyel lain down on his mat when the witch woke up and went to where she had hidden her huge, sharp knife. This time, Fereyel said nothing. Debbo Engal crept out of the hut and into the largest building in her compound. With the quickness brought by long experience, she moved stealthily among the sleeping forms, killing the ten who were covered with white robes. Then she returned to her hut, excited by the thought of the splendid meal that she would enjoy the next morning.

Once the witch was asleep, Fereyel again crept back to the big hut and awoke his brothers. As soon as they saw what had happened and Fereyel explained who had murdered the young women, the brothers began to run for home.

When Debbo Engal awoke, she hurried to the hut to prepare her fiendish breakfast, only to find out that she had killed her daughters by mistake and that the brothers were all gone. In a fury she commanded the wind to come to her and she climbed upon it and rode it toward the brothers' home.

When Fereyel saw the witch coming, he cried out to the brothers to beware. They did not know what to do, but Fereyel did. He found a hen's egg under a bush, and he threw it on the ground between the fleeing brothers and the witch. The smashed egg turned into a wide river that the witch could not pass. However, she pulled out a magic calabash and soon bailed all of the water out of the deep river so that she was able to pursue the brothers again.

Once more Fereyel saw Debbo Engal approaching, and he picked up a large rock, which he threw between the brothers and the witch. The rock was transformed into a high mountain that Debbo Engal could not climb. The witch was not ready to give up yet, though. Now she pulled out a magic axe and chopped her way through the mountain. Unluckily for her, it took her too long to do so, for the brothers managed to reach their home a step ahead of her and she was unable to capture them.

The next morning the brothers were asked by the village headman to go into the bush to gather firewood. They did so hesitantly, fearful that Debbo Engal was still after them, and it was true—she had heard the headman ask them to gather firewood and had turned herself into a log. Fereyel, though, realized what she had done, and he warned his brothers, who managed to run home before the witch could change back into her normal form and chase them.

The witch was not about to give up. A few days later when the brothers were sent to gather wild plums, they found that all of the bushes but one had died. That one bush had bright green leaves and its branches were filled with sweet, juicy plums. Fereyel again realized that this was a trick of the witch's, who had changed herself into the bush in order to trap them, and the brothers again escaped. Still another morning the brothers got up to find a donkey grazing outside their hut. All of them but Fereyel climbed upon its back to have a ride, but, as small as he was, there was not enough room for him to join them. When he mentioned this, the donkey suddenly grew longer. "I don't think that I would like to ride on a donkey with such a long back," he said. As soon as these words were uttered, the donkey shrank to its original size. "You have been tricked again," said Fereyel. "The donkey is none other than the witch." The brothers jumped off the donkey's back and ran home to the safety of their hut.

By now the witch realized that the only way that she could capture the brothers was to catch Fereyel first. So, the next morning she arrived at the village in the guise of a beautiful maiden. She sought out Fereyel and told him that she had come to visit him. Fereyel entertained the lovely woman in the visitors' hut, giving her the meat of a young goat that he had killed for his mother to cook. As dusk came, the young maiden asked Fereyel to help her find her way back home in the dark bush. Fereyel agreed to accompany her. The couple had not ventured far into the bush before the maiden stepped behind a large tree and then emerged a moment later, having changed into a monstrous python that charged straight at Fereyel. Fereyel had been waiting for something like this to happen, and as soon as the snake started toward him, he changed himself into a roaring fire and quickly the python was burned completely to ashes.

Fereyel returned to his village and told his brothers and the towns-people what had happened. That night there was great feasting and wild, festive dancing as all of the townspeople celebrated Fereyel's victory over Debbo Engal, the wicked witch.

How the Ashanti Became Debtors

G H A N A

*I*n Ghana the Ashanti people tell
the story of "How the Ashanti Became Debtors" to explain
the origin of this practice.

How the Ashanti Became Debtors

*O*ne day a hunter named Soko traveled from the town of Mina into the country of the Ashanti. He soon became friendly with the Ashanti people and felt at home among them. Indeed, he even married an Ashanti woman from Komasi.

Although he lived with the Ashanti for many years, there was still one thing that set Soko apart from his neighbors: since he had first arrived, he had been in debt. This bothered the Ashanti because none of them had ever owed anybody anything. After a while, the elders discussed the situation. Finally, they decided to send some of the old men to talk to Soko.

"Soko, you are our friend. But, we are very bothered by the fact that you owe some money. Before you arrived here, no one in the Ashanti owed anybody anything. You must find a way to rid yourself of your debt."

Soko took what they said to heart. He thought long and hard about what to do. He agreed that he must rid himself of his debt, yet he could think of no way to do this. Then, one day while Soko was in the forest making palm wine, he saw Anansi, the spider.

"Anansi, my friend, you are known to be very intelligent," he said. "I have a problem; maybe you can help me."

"Soko, you are my friend. Tell me what your problem is. Perhaps I can help you with it."

"I thank you, my friend. You see, I owe some money from very long ago, and I do not know how to get rid of my debt."

Anansi pondered for some time.

"Well," he said, "you need to give the debt to someone else. Possibly you can just make a bargain. You can say, 'Whoever drinks this palm wine assumes my debt.'"

"That sounds like a very good idea," Soko replied. "Whoever drinks this palm wine assumes my debt."

Slyly Anansi said, "Now maybe you will let me sample the palm wine that you are making."

"Why, of course. Take as much as you like," Soko said with barely disguised glee. Anansi cheerfully helped himself to the palm wine, for this was what he had really wanted from the beginning.

Soko jumped up and down. "Whosoever drinks this palm wine assumes my debt," he shouted happily. "Ha! Now I don't have the debt anymore! It is yours!"

Anansi took the debt and went back to his farm, where he planted some *Kaffir* corn.[1] "Whosoever eats my corn assumes my debt," Anansi announced. The corn grew to maturity. One day a bird stopped and ate some of the corn. "Whosoever eats this corn assumes my debt," Anansi shouted. "Now I don't have the debt anymore! It is yours!"

The bird flew back into the forest. Soon she built a nest and laid some eggs in it. "Whosoever breaks my eggs assumes my debt," she said. That afternoon while the bird was away from the nest, the wind came up and shook the branches of the tree. The eggs fell out of the nest and broke. When the bird returned, she exclaimed, "Whosoever breaks my eggs assumes my debt! Now I don't have the debt anymore! It is yours!"

In the spring the tree, which had assumed the debt, grew blossoms on her branches. "Whosoever eats my blossoms assumes my debt," she said. It was not long before a monkey visited the tree and made a lunch of the tasty, delicate blossoms. The tree said, "Whosoever eats my blossoms assumes my debt. Now I don't have the debt anymore! It is yours!"

The monkey swung to another tree. As he swung through the air, the monkey shouted, "Whosoever eats me assumes my debt." A lion

---

1. *Kaffir corn,* millet or sorghum.

who had been sleeping under the tree was awakened by the monkey's chatter. With one leap he grabbed the monkey and ate him. The monkey cried, "Whosoever eats me assumes my debt. Now I don't have the debt anymore! It is yours!"

"Wah," the lion roared, "Whosoever eats me assumes my debt."

One morning while Soko was hunting in the forest he came upon the lion. After a fierce battle, he killed the lion. As was the custom, Soko took the meat back to the village and shared it with the people there. When they ate the lion's meat, the Ashanti people assumed the debt, and they have never been able to be rid of debt since.

How Humankind Came to Have Talking Drums

*T*hroughout West Africa talking drums have been used as a means of communication for many generations. Typically, a talking drum is a two-headed, hourglass-shaped drum that is carried. The drummer, beating the instrument with a curved stick, is able to produce sounds of various lengths and tones that to some extent mimic human speech. The sound can carry great distances.

This story is told among the Wala people of northern Ghana.

How Humankind Came to Have Talking Drums

Long ago the guinea fowl, who was named MnMmengu, and the hawk, who was called Setu, were best friends. Then one day the two birds had a falling out.

The hawk had asked the guinea fowl to help him make some talking drums so that they could dance the *dogho*.[1] The two friends went into the bush, where they cut down a large oak tree. From the wood of this tree they carved their talking drums. While the drums were sitting in the sun to dry, the guinea fowl asked the hawk to watch over them. However, as it was lunchtime, the hawk was hungry and wanted to go home to eat.

"If the drums become dried before I return," the hawk said to the guinea fowl, "please wait until I get back before you beat them. Otherwise there will be a great *palava*[2] between us."

"I will do as you wish, my friend," replied the guinea fowl.

The hawk flew off to seek his lunch. While he was gone, the talking drums finished drying in the heat of the sun. The guinea fowl touched the drums to see if they were dry. As he touched them, they began to talk. The guinea fowl was pleased, and he began to beat them harder and harder.

First, he made a sound like his own name, MnMmengu. "MnMmengu, MnMmengu, MnMmengu," called the drums. Next, the guinea fowl made the drums sing the name of his friend, Setu.

"Setu, Setu, Setu," spoke the drums.

---

1. *Dogho,* a ritual dance.
2. *Palava,* trouble.

MnMmengu was very pleased, and as he beat the drums he became more and more excited. Soon he was beating out both his own name and his friend's name:

MnMmengu, Setu, MnMmengu, Setu.
MnMmengu, MnMmengu.
Setu, Setu.
MnMmengu, Setu, MnMmengu, Setu.

At this point the hawk, who was just finishing his lunch, heard the drums talking. He immediately began the flight back to the bush. In the meantime, the guinea fowl kept beating the drums. As for the hawk, the more he heard the drums talking and the closer he got to them, the madder he became. In fact, he grew so angry and he flew so fast that he flew right past the guinea fowl, who was still beating the drums. The guinea fowl thought that the speed of the hawk's flight meant that Setu was sharing in MnMmengu's joy. He beat the drums again and again:

MnMmengu, Setu, MnMmengu, Setu.

The now livid Setu thought that he was being taunted by his former friend and he wheeled around and flew low and fast. As he neared the guinea fowl, he screamed in anger and reached forward with his talons to cut off MnMmengu's head. Hearing the hawk's scream and seeing the sharp talons aimed at him, the guinea fowl ran into the bush as fast as he could to escape his former friend. From that day until this, hawks and guinea fowl have been enemies.

Fortunately, the hawk and the guinea fowl were so intent on each other that when they left the talking drums they never returned for them, and the people of a nearby village took the drums home with them. They used them to accompany the *dogho* dance and to communicate with the peoples of other villages, and they still use talking drums to do these things today.

Why Humans Die

*M*yths relating to the origin of
the universe and its constituent parts, including the earth
and humanity, are found in all cultures. The various myths
contained in West African folklore contain many elements
that are common to most origin stories, as well as some elements that are unique. "Why Humans Die" is a story told
among the Kono people of Guinea.

Why Humans Die

In the beginning of the world there was nothing but darkness. Sa (death), his wife, and their daughter lived in this dark world. Because they needed somewhere to live, Sa used his magic to create a huge ocean of mud where the family lived for many years.

One day God, who was called Alatangana, decided to visit Sa. When he arrived, God was appalled by the dirty world in which Sa and his family lived.

"Sa," said God, "how can you live in such a dirty place? You have created a world without plants or any living creatures. You have created a place where there is not even any light. Something must be done about this."

God began by making the huge ocean of mud solid. Because he loved life and found Sa's world barren, he created all of the kinds of plants and animals that exist.

Sa was greatly pleased by Alatangana's improvements of his world, and he and God entered into a great friendship.

God, who had no wife, found Sa's daughter very attractive. He asked Sa for his daughter's hand in marriage. Sa, however, did not wish for his daughter to leave his household, and he refused God's request.

God and the young daughter decided to be married anyway. God did not even offer to pay Sa the bride price that custom requires. Once Alatangana and Sa's daughter made this decision, they knew that Sa would be very angry, so they moved away to the farthest corner of the earth. For many years the couple lived happily, and they had fourteen children, seven boys and seven girls. Four of the boys and four of the girls were white, and the other three boys and girls were black. The family was not completely happy, though, because the children spoke among themselves in languages that

God and his wife did not understand. God became angry at this situation and he decided to palaver[1] with Sa to see whether his father-in-law knew the cause of this incredible situation.

When God reached Sa's home, Sa spoke with much animosity. "The reason that your children speak different languages from you and their mother is because I wished to punish you for your offense in stealing my daughter. You will never understand the words of your children."

God was astounded.

Sa continued, "Nevertheless, you will find that I am not completely hard-hearted. I shall give your children presents. To some children I will give intelligence and paper and ink so that they may record what they think. To other children I will give everything that they need to feed and protect themselves—the hoe, the machete, and the axe. Furthermore, I would recommend that the white children marry only among themselves and that the black children do likewise."

Because he wanted to become friends again with his father-in-law, God agreed with all that Sa said. When he returned home, he arranged the marriages of all of his children and sent them to all of the areas of the world where the white and black races would evolve. God's children were the ancestors of those white peoples we now call the French, English, Irish, Italians, Germans, Spanish, Polish, and so forth; they were also the ancestors of those black people who we now call the Kono, Guuerze, Manon Malinke, Toma, and Yacouba.

Unfortunately, even though the world was now full of plants, animals, and humans, it was still a place of darkness. Again God sought Sa's advice. He asked the *tou-tou*[2] and the rooster to fly to Sa's abode to find out what might be done. He gave them money and food for their journey and sent them on their way. When the *tou-tou* and the rooster arrived at Sa's abode and explained their mission, Sa said to

---

1. *Palaver,* to have a discussion or debate.
2. *Tou-tou,* a small red bird that is an early riser.

them, "Come in. I will teach each of you a song that you can use to bring forth the light of day. Then the people can go about their work in daylight rather than in darkness." When the *tou-tou* and the rooster returned and told God what Sa had done, God became very angry because he did not understand how singing a song could do any good. "In spite of the provisions I gave you for your journey, you did not do as I asked. You deserve to die." Still, God was merciful and he forgave the two birds.

Soon, first the *tou-tou* and then the rooster began to sing. Barely had the two begun their song when the daylight of the first dawn appeared. As Sa had commanded, the sun rose on the horizon and began its daily trip across the heavens. At the end of the day, the sun went to his bed on the other side of the world. As the sun did this, the moon and stars began to appear in the sky because Sa wished that there should be some light even at night. And, from that day until this, first the *tou-tou* and then the rooster must sing in the morning to bring forth the light.

Sa now visited Alatangana. "You did me a great disservice. You stole my only child. In spite of this, I have been your friend; I have given you the sun and the moon and the stars. I think that now you should do something for me."

God answered, "What is your wish, my father-in-law?"

"As you have taken my child, so must you give me one of yours. You must do this whenever I ask you to give me one. Each child that I call will hear a calabash rattle in his dreams."

God was very saddened, but he realized that he owed Sa a great debt and that he had transgressed in taking Sa's daughter without paying the bride price. Thus it is that ever since, human beings have had to die.

The Hunter and the Boa Constrictor

I V O R Y   C O A S T

*T*he folklore of many cultures contains dilemma tales, *stories meant to raise an intellectual question to be discussed by the listeners. Because the intent is to raise questions rather than provide answers, sometimes the protagonist is left in the throes of the dilemma when the tale ends. "The Hunter and the Boa Constrictor" contains many elements found in similar tales from other cultures, including a captured animal granting wishes in exchange for its freedom. This tale is told in the Ivory Coast.*

The Hunter and the Boa Constrictor

*O*nce upon a time there was a very poor man, a hunter, who was unable to catch any prey with his bent-wood and reed traps. When he set his traps in the savannah, he caught nothing. When he moved his traps to the forest, he still caught nothing. Even when he set his traps in the trees to try to capture birds or in the river to try to catch fish, the birds and fish avoided them and the traps remained unsprung.

One morning, just when the hunter was running out of patience and beginning to wonder where he might set his snares next, he visited his traps and found that he had captured a boa constrictor. The surprised man was about to kill the large snake with his spear when the boa cried out, "Oh, please do not kill me, mighty hunter!"

The hunter was startled. "Why should I not kill you?" he asked. "When your people catch a man, they always kill him."

"Dear hunter," said the snake in what he hoped was a reasonable tone, "have I ever wronged anyone in your family?"

The hunter replied that none of his family had ever been killed by a boa constrictor.

"Let me go, then. I know that it has been many months since you have caught anything in your traps and that you are a very poor man. If you free me, I will make you richer than the singing of it."

The hunter sat down to think about the snake's proposal. After a while he said, "If I kill you, then I can sell your skin and dry your meat and I will become well-to-do. Besides, you are a snake. How do I know that you will not try to cheat me? Once I let you go, you might not make me rich after all. Prepare to die." He raised his spear.

"No," said the snake anxiously. "Please do not kill me. I promise that I will make you the richest man alive." The boa constrictor looked at the hunter. "It's your choice. You can be rich or you can remain poor and continue to lead a wretched life."

The hunter put down his spear and released the snake from the trap.

"Thank you. Now, follow me. You will see that we animals are not as devious as you men."

The man followed the boa. Ultimately, they reached the snake's village, where the hunter remained for some time. When he was finally ready to leave, the boa gave him two small gourds.

"Follow my directions carefully, and do exactly what I say," said the snake. "As soon as you get back to your village, throw one gourd to the ground, but keep the other one because as long as you have it, you will be able to understand all of the languages spoken on earth."

The hunter eagerly took the two gourds and ran back to his home village, for he was afraid that the boa might change its mind. As soon as he reached his home, the hunter threw one of the gourds to the ground. Immediately, a huge castle appeared, filled with riches beyond the singing of it. For many years the hunter lived happily, frequently reminding himself, "If I had killed that fine boa because I was poor, that would have been a terrible mistake. Sometimes it is better not to listen to one's fears and hungers, for if I had done so, I would not be blessed with all of these riches."

One day the hunter's dog brought home a mangy dog that had no master. While the two dogs were eating lunch, the mangy dog forecast, "In two moons there will be a great famine. If someone heard me telling you this, they could become quite wealthy."

The hunter, who had been eating his lunch as well, overheard the two dogs talking. Of course, he could understand what they said since he had used the boa's gourds as he had been instructed. As soon as he could, the man visited the village market and bought everything edible that had been harvested. He placed all of these foodstuffs in a special hut and waited for two months. As predicted, the famine arrived. The hunter, who possessed the only food for sale in his town, sold it all at a very dear price. As a result, he became many times richer than he had been before.

Soon afterwards, the mangy dog visited the hunter's house again. "Ah," the mangy dog said to his friend, "I see that one man's misery can be another man's blessing. Still, if your master only knew what was to come, he would not be so happy with his riches."

"Why? What is to come?"

"In one moon, all of the young women of the village will die of the plague unless they move to the other side of the river."

The hunter, who once again had heard the dogs talking, quickly had a beautiful home built on the other side of the river. No sooner was it built than he moved his family across the river to live. As prophesied by the mangy dog, a plague arrived at the village shortly and destroyed the lives of all of the young girls who lived there. When the plague had run its course, the hunter and his family moved back to the village. Because his daughters were the only young women still alive in the village, they were soon taken as wives by the young men, and since he was now father-in-law of all of these young men, his riches increased even more.

On another occasion, the mangy dog predicted that a fire would destroy the village and everything in it, including his friend's master's fortune. Naturally, because the hunter had understood what the mangy dog said, he moved his valuables before the terrible fire broke out. Thus, he saved everything.

The next time the mangy dog visited, he said to his friend, "I believe that your master understands our language."

"But men cannot understand animals! Why would you say that?"

"Because every time I have told you about a forthcoming calamity, your master has known what to do to avoid it. However, next week there will be a flood worse than any other yet seen in this country."

As might be guessed, once more the hunter understood what was said and he managed to prepare for the flood in time to protect all of his goods. Even the hunter's dog was beginning to be convinced that his master could understand what the mangy dog said to him.

By now it had been twenty years since the hunter had released the boa constrictor and received the gourds in return. One last time the mangy dog visited the home of the hunter. When he saw the hunter's dog he said, "Your master's going to die."

"When is this going to happen?"

"He's going to die exactly at noon today."

"Is there any way that he can save himself?"

"He can continue to live if he takes the remaining gourd back to the boa. If he does this, however, he will become poor again, poorer than ever. He will have to become a hunter once more. He will live for a very long time but only in the poorest of conditions. It is a decision that he will have to make."

As before, the hunter overheard the dogs talking. He was dumbfounded. It was only morning, so there were several hours left for him to make his decision. But, oh, what a decision! Would it be better to die happy now, or to live a long, wretched life? Which would you choose?

Spider and Monkey
Go to a Feast

*O*f all of the animals in West African folktales, Spider and Monkey are among the characters who appear most frequently. In "Spider and Monkey Go to a Feast," Spider's gluttony and selfishness are pitted against Monkey's quick wit. This story, told to Edward W. Smith by his grandmother, is one of the most ubiquitous in Liberian society. It is frequently told to youngsters in many tribal groups and thus exists in an untold number of versions. The following version is among the shortest and least complicated of them.

Spider and Monkey Go to a Feast

*O*nce upon a time, Spider and Monkey were very good friends, so much so that they did everything together. One day Spider heard about a feast that some townspeople were having at the bottom of the River Ces. Because of Spider's excessive fondness for food, he decided to attend. There was one problem with Spider's plan, however; he could not swim. Thus, he decided to play a trick on Monkey.

Spider invited Monkey to go to the feast with him. Monkey agreed under one condition—that Spider would permit him to eat as much as he wanted. Spider agreed, and they set out for the river.

When Spider and Monkey reached the edge of the river, Monkey told his friend to put on an overcoat filled with rocks so that Spider could sink to the bottom of the water. When they reached the bottom of the river, Spider was ready to play his trick. He said to the townspeople, "Before anyone starts eating, his hands should be washed clean." He knew very well that the dark palms of Monkey's hands would remain black.[1] Spider thought that he had surely tricked Monkey. But, no sooner had Spider sat down to eat than Monkey said that all of those wearing overcoats should take them off, and when Spider removed his rock-filled coat, up he floated to the top of the river before he had eaten a bite.

---

1. The component of Monkey being unable to remove the black color from his palms appears in other West African folktales. In a story told by the Mpongwe people of Equatorial West Africa (now Gabon), for instance, Tortoise invites the animals to a feast and declares that they must all wash their hands with soap before eating from the common serving bowls (the custom was to eat with one's hands, without utensils). Because Monkey's hands remain black, the other animals will not let him eat.

Why Beavers Eat Crabs

*I*n many folktales from "prehis-
toric" or preliterate times, it is assumed that all animals,
including humans, lived in a common society. Stories
about talking animals are often used to illustrate concepts that are applicable to human behavior.

"Why Beavers Eat Crabs" is a Gio story presented by
Alfred Slueh Barbley. The Cavalla River forms part of
the eastern border of Liberia and runs through the land
where the Gio live.

Why Beavers Eat Crabs

There lived in the Cavalla River near the town of Druborh three friends: Beaver, Rock, and Crab. All of them had known each other from the very beginning of the settlement.

Beaver was one of Druborh's richest citizens. He owned large stores where all kinds of goods were sold. Everybody in the town did business with him.

Rock and Crab were inhabitants of the town as well. They were friendly with Beaver. They worked for him every once in a while to earn a little money for their respective families.

One day Rock thought of a plan to get money from Beaver. He went to Beaver and said, "Oldman[1] Beaver. You know, I want to borrow some money from you—about two hundred dollars. I will pay you when I get bigger. You see, family palava[2] gives me a hard time."

It is well known that it takes hundreds of years for a rock to accumulate material in order to grow in size. Rock's intention was to delay in repaying Beaver. Since Beaver was not familiar with the growth process of rocks, he consented to Rock's proposed plan and gave him the money.

Rock took the money and started improving his standing in the community. He started a farm where he planted crops. He also began sending his children to school.

To keep Beaver from growing suspicious of him, Rock often visited his friend to discuss pertinent questions of the day.

Beaver observed the size of Rock as the years went by. He finally realized that Rock was not increasing in size at all. One day Beaver

---

1. *Oldman,* a term of respect denoting knowledge.
2. *Palava,* trouble.

decided to discuss the situation with Crab. Up to this time, Crab had been jealous about the progress that Rock was making in the community. He had even tried to think of a way to get Rock in trouble and thereby thwart Rock's plans for further development.

When Beaver mentioned the money business[3] to Crab, Crab saw an opportunity to spoil Rock's plans. He told Beaver that Rock was deceiving him. He explained the growth process of Rock to Beaver. When Beaver learned that he had been tricked, he became very angry. He decided to deal harshly with Rock.

That evening Rock went to visit Beaver as usual, but this time Beaver's response was decidedly cool. Beaver said, "You deceiver, do not call me Oldman anymore. Am I wiser than you? I learned that this is your usual size. You just want to use my money while I'm alive, without paying me. Then when I die you will go free with my money-o!"[4] Beaver went on to say, "Crab has just been here with me. He told me about your growth process. You know that Crab knows all about you. Do you want to tell me he is lying?"

In reply Rock said, "Oldman, you know what? It is true that Crab is my friend. He knows more about me than you do, but he has misinformed you this time. I have been thinking about repaying you in the next few months. Really, it has been for Crab's sake that I have been kept from repaying you. He borrowed the money from me and bought that fine shell that is on his back. You may have noticed that for the past few days his shell has been shining more brightly than before. When he comes here, ask him." Beaver's anger subsided.

The next day, Crab went to visit Beaver again, this time expecting to get a reward for having revealed Rock's secret. When Beaver saw Crab's shining shell, he was furious. In his rage Beaver grabbed Crab by the shell and tore him to pieces. In fact, he ate Crab. And, that is why beavers eat crabs today.

---

3. *Business,* problem.
4. An "o" at the end of a word serves as an exclamation, a way of adding emphasis.

The Fish Who Was Visited by a Baby Star

L I B E R I A

*F*rom Yawuahun clan chief Watson in Loffa County in Liberia, Joseph Brent heard the story "The Fish Who Was Visited by a Baby Star." This simple parable is about knowing one's place and manners, though Brent felt that the tale also concerns the "nature of good and bad."

The Fish Who Was Visited by a Baby Star

A baby star came down from the heavens one night to bathe in a pond of sweet water. A little fish was swimming about in the pond, looking here and there for things to eat. He was surprised when he found the star bathing in the pond, but he politely greeted the visitor and asked, "Oh star, my pond is such a small and unimportant pond. Why did you choose to come here?"

"No special reason," said the star. "The water here is clear and sweet, and I am only a baby star." And then, thinking that the fish was a simpleton, he added, "Tell me, will the moon bathe in the sea tonight?"

"I will be happy to tell you," answered the little fish, "but first you must tell me why one of my crabs lives with a water-snail."

The baby star laughed at such foolishness. "How stupid you are," he said. "I live up in the sky. What do I know of such things?"

"And you are two fools," the little fish declared, "for I live in this pond, and what do I know of the sky, or the moon, or if she will bathe in the sea tonight?"

The little star blushed with shame and flew away.

Gboloto, the River Demon

In the town of Folah in Bong County (which is situated in north-central Liberia), an elder of the Kpelle tribe related to Freddie Yancy this story of a daughter who lies to her mother and undergoes a trial by ordeal.

Gboloto, the River Demon

*O*nce long ago in the Kpelle country there was a village surrounded by a river. In this river there lived a demon, called Gboloto, who swallowed people who lied. Anyone suspected of lying was placed on the river in a skillet. Gboloto would swallow those who had lied.

Now, a mother, her two daughters, and their cat lived in this village. Every day when the big sister cooked, she would place her mother's rice, peppers, and cassava food on the table. They were a happy family and things were going well, when something happened that spoiled the peace of their home. One day when the mother came home from work, some of the food had disappeared from the bowls.

The mother asked what was happening to the food, but the girls both said that they didn't know.

One day the little girl's mouth was all covered with oil. The mother called the girl to her and asked if she had been taking the food. "No, no," the girl exclaimed, "it is big sister who takes the food-o!" Naturally, the big sister swore that she knew nothing about her mother's missing food.

The next day the mother pretended to go to work but stayed at home. After the older girl had dished up the dinner, the mother stood behind the dining room door to see who would steal some of the food. As she stood there, the older girl came, took some meat, and ate it. The mother went out and returned in the evening. She called the older girl and questioned her again. Still the big sister denied even touching the food.

"I know what I'll do. I'll take you all to Gboloto," said the overwrought mother.

Early the next morning they all went to the waterside where the small girl was the first to get into the frying pan. When the pan was pushed onto the water, she began singing this song:

Ma, if that is me eat
the rice and the soup, fry pan
must carry me down and
Gboloto must swallow me.

After singing this song three times she was removed from the skillet. Then the big sister was put into the pan. As the older sister sang, the skillet began to sink in the water, carrying her down. When the water reached her waist, her mother asked her if she was willing to confess, but she still denied that she had stolen the food. She started singing again. The water covered her up to her throat. Still, she would not tell the truth, so the water covered her completely. Gboloto had again caught its victim.

The mother and the little girl turned and went up the hill to their home, where they lived happily ever after. They may still be there, if you want to check for them.

Gonotee

*T*he Kpelle tale "Gonotee" was told to Q. Saye Guah by his grandfather. Guah was born in the town of Geh, near which the Geno Creek runs. "Gonotee" is an explanation of why a specific part of the creek is considered sacred even today.

Gonotee

There was a man in Geh whose name was Gonotee. One day he went fishing on the Geno, a little creek not far from the town.

While walking in the water, Gonotee came to a place where there was a waterfall. Green moss had grown on the rocks around the fall, and this made them very slippery. As he was slowly trying to walk over the rocks, Gonotee slipped and fell into the waterfall. To his surprise, he found himself in a cave surrounded by rocks. He looked around the cave carefully. Then he climbed out of the cave.

One morning Gonotee left to visit his new discovery without informing anyone in the town. He returned the next day and told his wife that he had been visiting his people under the Geno. His wife was very puzzled.

Within two days the news of Gonotee's visit to his people who had died long ago and now lived under the water of the Geno spread far and near. In fact, Gonotee took many people to the waterfall to see him plunge into it. The people began to regard him as a great "water medicine man." He claimed to be able to heal all sicknesses that were caused by violations of the tribe's water rules.

Gonotee jealously guarded his newly discovered power. He told the people that anyone who fell in the area around the mouth of the cave would automatically be transformed into a member of the opposite sex. Children were seriously advised by parents not even to go close to that part of the forest where Gonotee's hidden place was.

Now and then Gonotee told the townspeople to make a sacrifice to the water people. Sometimes he would ask for chickens, rice, palm oil, and vegetables. Whatever he would ask for, the people would give him. He would take these into the cave and feast on them. Sometimes he spent several weeks in the cave. When he returned, he brought what he called messages from the water people to the townspeople. He would tell them that their relatives under the water said hello.

Gonotee did all sorts of things to make the people believe that water people lived in the waterfall. Some days he would dress like a woman and sit on a rock near the waterfall. As soon as he saw anyone, he would plunge into the water and disappear.

Besides the gifts that were meant for the water people, Gonotee received many personal gifts. People brought him chickens, goats, rice, palm oil, and even sows. He became very rich, and he even built his own town. So, Gonotee remained a great waterman until his death. Even after his death, the people still considered the place near the waterfall prohibited. They told their children about the great waterman, Gonotee. Their children in those days believed them, for when the old people said that Gonotee went underwater even during the rainy season when the water got deeper, no one doubted it.

The underwater cave remained a secret for many years. Then one day a group of daring schoolboys went fishing in the Geno Creek. When they got to the waterfall, one of the boys said, "One of these days I shall jump right into this waterfall." Another brave boy replied, "Let's jump into it now-o!"

The boys jumped into the waterfall and found themselves at the mouth of the cave. To their surprise they saw that the cave was cut in such a way that no matter how high the water in the creek rose, none of it ever entered the cave.

After this, the boys made many visits to the cave. They even cooked and ate there. They told many people about the cave and how Gonotee had lied to them, but the old folk would not believe them. Even today the townspeople make sacrifices on Geno Creek by Gonotee's waterfall.

The Two Brothers

*C*ombining the theme of a spir-
it's preference for the younger of two brothers and a dream
vision, "Two Brothers" is another tale of the Kpelle people in
Liberia. It was related by Kojo H. Woods.

The Two Brothers

*F*ar back in an African village on a farm near the Pore River there lived a man, his wife, and their two sons. Every day the two boys asked their father for permission to go and swim in the river when the sun got very hot.

At the river the younger brother often took his father's canoe and went far out to the deepest part of the river. One day he went farther out than usual. Finally, he got to a spot where there were many large rocks, and on top of one of the rocks he found a comb. This comb was quite ornately decorated, so the boy decided to take the comb home with him. He took the comb to the shore of the river, but he did not tell his older brother what he had found.

While the boy was asleep that night a beautiful woman appeared to him and asked him for the comb. She told him that while she was combing her hair that morning she had accidentally left it on the rock. She promised to give him anything he wanted, if only he would permit her to take her comb back to the river.

The boy thought this over for a while and decided to give her the comb, but without asking for anything special. He told her that he would be grateful for anything that she felt like giving him.

In return for his kindness the beautiful woman promised the boy that he would become a wise man and the leader of his tribal people. Folk from all around his village, even many from beyond, would love him and give him many valuable gifts, she said.

After four or five years things began to work out as the woman had promised. All of the people began to love the young man, and at a very early age he became chief of the village. His parents were extremely happy and proud of their son, but his elder brother was jealous and began to say evil things about him.

One day the elder brother went to a sand cutter[1] to find out why his smaller brother had become so great and famous. The fortune teller told him about the comb and the beautiful woman, but he did not reveal that his brother had refused to request any special thing from the woman. The older brother hurriedly ran to the river, took the canoe, and went to the identical spot where the precious comb had been found. On the same rock he, too, found a comb. It was through some magic played by the fortune teller that the comb had been placed on the rock, although the older brother did not know this.

He was the very first to go to bed that night, but he was only to be disappointed because the beautiful woman did not appear. In fact, for over ten years he kept the comb by his bed, but no one ever came for it.

The older brother's jealousy grew stronger and stronger. Finally, he realized that he would never see the beautiful woman and have his wishes fulfilled; he decided to kill his brother. The night before he was going to commit the murder, the beautiful woman came while the jealous brother slept and killed him. He died a bitter, poor man, and his evil plan to get even with his brother was never realized.

---

1. *Sand cutter,* a fortune teller.

The Devil and Her Daughter

LIBERIA

*E*xplanations of where animals come from constitute an important category in folklore. How snails evolved is the focus of "The Devil and Her Daughter," a fanciful Kpelle tale told by Moses S. Flumo.

The Devil and Her Daughter

Once upon a time there lived a man and his wife in a little country town. They had not been married long when the woman became pregnant. After a few months, the husband walked off for some reason or the other. Angry and frustrated because her husband had deserted her, the woman also left the town and went into the bush to settle somewhere on a farm all by herself. She did not intend to return to town ever again. Over the months she got used to the ways of the bush and became very much afraid of human beings. After a time she became as wild as the beasts of the forest. She struggled all by herself and gave birth to a girl child, who she named Korlu.

Though Korlu's mother had become wild, Korlu remained normal and maintained all of the characteristics typical of human beings. Furthermore, Korlu grew up to be beautiful beyond belief. One day Korlu's mother found a new site in the forest where she built a cabin in which they both lived.

Then came a time when Korlu's mother became very hairy and turned into a devil. She even developed wings and began to fly. She divided the cabin into two compartments, one of which she kept for herself and the other she assigned to Korlu.

The devil could not enter Korlu's compartment of the cabin, and Korlu could not enter the devil's because it was filled with human skulls. They shared only the living room of the cabin. The devil mother fed on human beings, while Korlu ate the meat of animals. During the day, Korlu's mother would go hunting for both human beings and animals, the human beings for her own food and the animals for Korlu's.

People from surrounding villages became very alarmed when they realized that the devil was destroying human beings. Nobody could go out into the forest in which they lived.

By this time Korlu had grown into an extremely beautiful woman in the forest. One day a handsome young man walked up to the cabin while the devil was out hunting. Korlu, who was always home when the devil went out to hunt, became interested in the young man at first sight, but she was afraid that her mother, the devil, would kill and devour him. Korlu warned the young man to leave immediately. He refused to go home, saying that he loved the beautiful Korlu and that he would not leave her alone in the forest. Korlu fell in love with the young man on the spot. She hid her lover in her compartment of the cabin and advised him not to say a word when her mother came home. When Korlu's mother got home, she asked Korlu if anyone had visited the cabin during her absence, but Korlu denied that there was anybody in the house. The devil was not pleased with this response at all.

When day broke, both Korlu and her lover decided to go together over to the fellow's hometown while the devil was away hunting. In the past the devil had taught Korlu all that she knew about jujus[1] and magical spells. Korlu took along some magic medicine in order to counteract anything that her mother might try to do to stop them from going.

As soon as the couple started off, the devil knew it and returned home in a great hurry. She dropped all that she brought and began chasing Korlu and her lover. But, whenever the devil used any magical spells that would hinder the young people in their journey, Korlu used a magical spell that counteracted her mother's. This went on throughout the journey until they were approaching the young man's town. At this point Korlu's mother had to return home because, as a devil, she could not enter a town of human beings. Korlu and her lover reached his home safely.

The devil, angered and frustrated for a second time, decided to go into the town after all and get her daughter, who was her only helper. The devil changed back into human form and went to the town. Before the devil could reach the town, however, Korlu knew that her mother would be coming to get her and when.

---

1. In West Africa a juju is an object used as a fetish or charm. During rituals, the priests or dancers often use juju bags, which are filled with such objects—feathers, bones, plants, and so forth. Sometimes the juju bag is kept in the mask worn for the ceremony.

Korlu's mother came to town and went directly to the home of Korlu and her lover. Korlu and the young man received the devil warmly. The devil already had decided to kill Korlu's lover in order to take her daughter back with her, but she did not betray her plan by her actions in any way. The devil slept in the town that night.

When day broke, she prepared to leave. She asked Korlu and her lover to escort her a few yards away from the town. She knew that once they left the town she might be able to kill Korlu's lover and take her daughter home to their cabin in the forest. Korlu, knowing what might happen on their way out of town, prepared to counter anything that her mother might do. Korlu prepared juju in the form of liquid and gave it to her lover.

When they got to a kola tree, Korlu's mother asked the young man to climb it and pick some kola nuts for her.[2] As he climbed into the tree, Korlu's mother changed into the devil again and began uttering magical words. While she said them, the tree got shorter and shorter until the very top stood only at ground level. Korlu in turn reversed the spell and the tree grew taller again. Back and forth the battle between the devil mother and her daughter raged, the tree getting alternately shorter and taller, depending on whose spell was stronger. After a long struggle, Korlu remembered the liquid juju that she had prepared for the young man. When the tree grew shorter again, Korlu told the young man to sprinkle the liquid on the devil. When he did so, the devil immediately turned into a big snail. Recognizing that she carried within her the seeds of her own destruction, in angry frustration she hissed through her teeth at the daughter, saying, "Behold what can kill a person is within his stomach."

This is said to be how snails evolved. Even today snails sound as though they are hissing through their teeth when they are disturbed suddenly.

---

2. Kola nuts are used to make beverages or medicine. Sometimes the leaves of the tree are chewed because they produce a slight narcotic effect.

The Underwater Home of the Ancestors

L I B E R I A

"The Underwater Home of the Ancestors" deals with the disappearance of the inhabitants of Gbedin, a town in Nimba County, and explains the relationship between the townspeople and one of their tribal ancestors. Wheyce Dolo Dokie, a member of the Mano tribe in the central Liberian town of Sanniquellie in Nimba County, narrated the tale to his nephew, Josephus S. Dokie.

The Underwater Home of the Ancestors

*O*nce there lived in Gbedin, a town in Nimba County near the St. John River, a palm wine tapper[1] named Saye. Saye's best palm tree overlooked the river and the town. When he was up in the tree, Saye could see the entire town.

One day Saye went to get a nip of his wine before noon. When he lifted the collecting gourd, it was completely empty. "Oh, has someone been here to steal the wine?" he thought aloud. He climbed down.

He went to town angry over the incident. "It could not be an ordinary passerby who just wanted a sip. It must be someone who wanted trouble," he thought. Saye decided to catch the thief. The next afternoon he returned earlier than usual and hid near the tree. He was determined to catch the robber in the act.

After a while he heard a noise from the river. He held his breath and watched keenly, like a hunter waiting for game. He saw an alligator transforming itself into a man. The alligator hid his skin under the palm leaves and climbed the palm tree.

Saye came out from his hiding place. He walked softly and carefully until he got to where the alligator-man had hidden its skin. Saye quickly grabbed the skin from under the palm leaves and ran to town.

The transformed man climbed down from the tree after he had sipped enough wine. He lifted the leaves to get his skin but it was not there. He looked all around; the skin was gone. He decided to go to town in search of his property.

---

1. Palm wine is distilled from the sap of the palm tree. The tapper climbs up the trunk of the tree and inserts a drain into it to collect the juice.

Gono, as the alligator-man was called, arrived at the town late in the afternoon. Some people directed him to the chief's compound. Gono called the chief aside and told him that he had to discuss a confidential matter. He openly confessed to the chief that he had lost an alligator skin. In fact, he said, he was one of the alligators that live in the St. John River. He promised that he would reward the whole town by protecting it in case of danger if the chief assisted him in finding the skin.

The chief decided to meet with the elders of the town. He ordered the town crier to announce an emergency meeting of all of the members of the Poro Society.[2]

All of the members assembled under the large cotton tree at the center of the town. The chief stood up and told them the purpose of the meeting. He asked the group about the skin. Saye admitted that he had the skin. He revealed to the group how he had gotten it. He promised to return the skin to its rightful owner.

Gono thanked the people of Gbedin. In revealing himself Gono said, "I am one of your ancestors who lives in the St. John River in the form of an alligator. Soon there will be a bitter land dispute between you and the neighboring town to the east, but fear not because under the St. John there is a large town that will be your sanctuary if you are ever in danger. Under the river, you will be able to reunite with your missing relatives. You are welcome always." He thanked the people of Gbedin once more and bade them farewell.

It was not long after Gono left that a bitter quarrel broke out between the people of Gbedin and the people of the neighboring town, just as the alligator-man had predicted. When the war became rough and there was no possibility of a compromise between the parties, the people of Gbedin gathered together all of their belongings and down they went under the St. John River. It is believed that the people of Gbedin are still under the river, for they never returned after the war.

---

2. *Poro Society*, the male secret society.

Zenneh and the Sacred River

If they are to fit into their society, the members of a culture must know and obey the group's social and religious rules. Transmittal of that knowledge and warnings about the consequences if it is ignored is a function of some folktales. An elder in the Mano tribe in Liberia's Nimba County recounted for Joseph Suah the story "Zenneh and the Sacred River," about the consequences of ignoring the group's social and religious rules.

Zenneh and the Sacred River

*A*mong the characteristics of African animalistic religions is the worship of idols—rivers, trees, and many other things found in the immediate environment. This tradition was clearly demonstrated by Zenneh, a lady who lived in the little village of Duogee Town in Nimba County in the early 1950s.

At that time there was a sacred river known as the Glayi in Duogee Town. The Glayi was extremely important in the lives of the inhabitants of Duogee Town, because it served as a source for their children. The men used to pray to the river for their wives to conceive babies. Since the river was considered highly sacred, the townspeople were prohibited from eating or drinking anything from it. This rule was passed on to strangers and is even taught to children born today.

One day, however, Zenneh, a beautiful woman in her thirties, decided to find out whether what she had been told about the river when she was a youth was actually true. So, she went fishing in the river one morning and caught a very big fish. She prepared a very delicious dumboy[1] and her entire family ate it mixed with a fish soup. The result was fatal. Everyone in the family took sick the next day and died. The children and their father never knew that the fish had come from the sacred river Glayi.

Then, less than a week later, the river mysteriously disappeared. By careful observation and study, the elders of the town discovered the reason for the river's disappearance. It was because Zenneh had violated the rules pertaining to the sacred river. Since that time, the spot where the Glayi used to run has remained just a sandy place.

---

1. *Dumboy,* a thick, sour paste made from pounded cassava or plantain and eaten on rice or served rolled into small balls that are swallowed whole.

One Great Fisherman

LIBERIA

"*O*ne Great Fisherman" was related by S. Folley Dunna of the Mano tribe in Grand Cape Mount County, located in central Liberia. The story is about a man's pride leading him to a destructive confrontation with the spirit world.

One Great Fisherman

*O*nce upon a time a fisherman named Jenekai lived in a little village not very far from the Mano River in Grand Cape Mount County, Liberia. Jenekai was born with a burning desire to become the greatest fisherman in his chiefdom. He was also the only child in his family.

Jenekai became such a successful and famous fisherman that no other fisherman could challenge him in the whole of Grand Cape Mount County. He was so courageous that he even decided to fish in an area of the Mano River that fishermen before him had avoided for ages because they believed that a powerful water spirit dwelt there.

When Jenekai decided to fish in that special spot, his family and the elders of both his village and the chiefdom warned him not to try that because they believed in the supernatural power of such terrific creatures as the water spirit. Still, his mind was set. Everyone was aware that Jenekai's death would be a great loss to all, particularly to his family, because he was the greatest man in his chiefdom and the only child of his family.

Finally, Jenekai made his first visit to that special part of the river. He caught many fish and returned safely. Over the next several months he made other visits and each time he returned without any difficulty, each time bringing back a great quantity of fish to feed all of the people of his village. The queerest thing about the spot was that Jenekai caught only one kind of fish there. This was queer because a number of different species of fish live in a large body of water such as a river, but the water spirit had bred this particular kind for centuries in that area and had driven all of the other fish away.

In time Jenekai's success cleared virtually all doubts about the danger of the river from the minds of his people. Then the water spirit decided to act.

One hot, sunny day Jenekai set out with a few other townsfolk under his direction to give the area of the spirit's home its final sweep. As usual, he took the lead when they arrived at the site. Suddenly, Jenekai disappeared under the river's water. The last thing that the others heard from him was his wailing voice crying out, "Carry the news to my people that the water spirit has captured me-o!" The water spirit had seized him and it never let him go. This was the end of Jenekai. When the news was carried back to his people, they were so sad that they mourned his loss for years.

The moral of this story is that it is always wise to take good advice, no matter how great one may be.

King Baboon and His Domain

L I B E R I A

*M*oses G. Bunnah related the
story called "King Baboon and His Domain." Like "One
Great Fisherman," this tale illustrates the impossibility of
bending nature or the spirits to one's will. In this case, however, an animal rather than a man is used to demonstrate
the mistake of hubris, or excessive pride that leads to over-
reaching oneself.

King Baboon and His Domain

*M*any years ago in the land of the land animals, Baboon, being the strongest of all of the animals, was crowned king by acclamation. Unfortunately, famine time came soon after this glorious event.

Everyone in Baboon's kingdom was growing more emaciated by the day as the supply of edible things grew thin and parents began to eat their own youngest and most unproductive children. The town's elders held a general council to ask the king to do something about their misery.

The council was brought to order, and King Baboon's booming voice rang out: "Fellow citizens, noble and honored guests, this famine, which has so destroyed our land, is the evil work of the angry god, Pelva. To appease Pelva, today we shall return home. Tomorrow each of us is to sacrifice to Pelva one *kinja*[1] of rice. On the next day each shall give a gourd[2] of palm oil, and on the third day two white and unblemished chickens shall be sacrificed to Pelva."

The order of the king was carried far and wide. After ten days had passed, there was no sign of the hunger ceasing. Therefore, the king gathered together all of his wise men and entreated them to consult their oracles in order to determine the causes of the terrible famine.

The wise men were given six days in which to bring back their findings. The chief diviner performed his ceremonies along with his assistants and came to the conclusion that the bad and hard time had been brought not by Pelva, but directly by Vinca, a sea monster. They recommended that in order for the famine to abate—yea, to be abolished, and the time of plenty restored—old Vinca had to be destroyed and the tears from her daughter's eyes used to fertilize the barren soil.

1. *Kinja,* a measure equivalent to about two cups.
2. *Gourd,* a measure equivalent to about one gallon.

King Baboon, having heard this, called his strong men to prepare two fleets of warships to sail to Dingby, where the monster lived. On the way the fleet foundered on the rocky shores of River Yak, and all but three of the 250-man army were killed. "Oh, King," declared the second-in-command, who had survived the rapids, "your bravest men have perished in the rough sea." Baboon became furious and ordered five more fleets to prepare to sail.

Within a month a 1,500-man army sailed for Dingby. After a journey of six weeks, the army reached Dingby but turned right back at the fearful sight of Vinca. The sea being very rough and almost impassable during this return trip, four of the five fleets were destroyed.

When he heard the news of the loss of his fleets, King Baboon became even more furious and lost his good judgment. He decided that if his men could not do this very important task, he, King Baboon, would do it. "I, King Baboon, King of the Animals, strongest of all, will destroy the monster Vinca, who has brought so much suffering to my people-o."

Baboon, with a mere one hundred men, set sail for Dingby, the home of the impossible possessor of two heads, one foot, one hundred eyes, one nose, two hundred fingers, and an enormous mouth that could swallow a blue whale. At the sight of Vinca, Baboon shot once and burst one of Vinca's eyes; he shot again, breaking three of the monster's fingers; and then he shot a third time but missed. When Baboon shot a fourth time, the bullet glanced off the impenetrable skin of Vinca and hit the king in his left shoulder. Seeing blood gushing from the felled king's deep wound, the men returned home. The king died the next morning.

The Farmer's Dream

*T*he history of Konsuo, an overly proud farmer who ultimately falls in a conflict between man and nature, is the subject of "The Farmer's Dream," recited by Ben Smallwood. The River Ya is located in north-central Liberia in the Mano tribe territory.

The Farmer's Dream

There lived, in a village near Lawalazu, a very poor farmer called Konsuo. Because of his poverty, Konsuo found it impossible to obtain more than one wife. Being embarrassed at having only one wife, Konsuo decided to take his spouse, leave the village, and rusticate on a farm that he made—the living conditions in his village had simply become unbearable for him. Konsuo left the village for the farm two days after he came to this decision.

While on the farm, the poor farmer and his wife did all of the work for themselves. While he cut and burned the farm,[1] she cooked sweet soup and rice for him every day.

One sunset after a hard day's work Konsuo came home and told his wife, "I have completed planting a large farm to feed us and still there will be plenty of rice left for us to sell. When we sell the rice, I will bring another wife to help you with all this hard work."

Konsuo and his wife worked day after day, caring for their rice farm and at the same time comforting one another as they looked forward to the day that they expected their farm to become prolific.

The growing season greeted the farmer's crops warmly at first, but before long a continuous rain came and destroyed a very large portion of the crops, leaving barely enough for Konsuo and his wife to eat. The farmer, however, considered the destruction of his crops to be a punishment inflicted upon him by some of his ancestors whom he had wronged while they were alive. To atone for the harm that he thought that he must have done, Konsuo visited the graves of his ancestors on seven consecutive nights to ask for forgiveness.

Time went by, and when the farmer felt that he had been forgiven, he decided to start another farm. He went to bed hoping to have a

---

1. The fields are burned to clear them of vegetation and enrich the soil before the rice is planted.

good dream about the size and shape of his new farm, but instead Konsuo dreamt a strange dream.

In this strange dream of his Konsuo found himself in an eerie, dark, highly forested, frightfully silent, unknown area. While he stood in the mist of darkness, silence, and loneliness, a bright light followed by a loud and masculine voice broke the darkness and the silence. In an authoritative tone the voice said, "Konsuo! You farmer! I, the father of nature and god of your father's gods, have destroyed your crops with water to test your faith in the gods of your father. This faith you have proven to have, for you did not curse the gods. You are a poor man with a strong desire to become rich one day, but if you want to get rich with cattle, goats, and sheep, and if you want people to honor you, you must behold the face of Suma, the god of wealth that lives across the Ya River. But, I must warn you," said the god of Konsuo's father's gods, "Ya is a very evil river that prevents people from seeing the face of Suma. Nevertheless, you can safely cross the river and return home if you do not become boastful."

Forgetting what the god told him about being a braggadocio, Konsuo told himself, "I have the strength of fifty bushcows. What can a small river like the Ya do to me? Anyway, what is water? It is a lazy, boneless, and weak running thing. I drink it every day. At times it may dislike the idea of my drinking it, but because it is so lazy, it says nothing to me. When it is in my body and wants to leave, it must ask my permission. I have no need to worry. I will beat that river with my small canoe by running through its heart like a sharp cutlass cutting through a banana."

When Konsuo awoke at the break of day, he told his wife what he had dreamed. Boastfully, he continued, "I, Konsuo, am going to do battle with the Ya today. That boneless and evil river that prevents one from becoming rich will lose its dignity to me by evening."

Feeling very confident, he shouldered his canoe, received a farewell smile from his wife, and headed for the river. Upon arriving at the river, Konsuo said aloud, "I have come to cross you and get rich-o!" Hurriedly he put his canoe into the river and started off, saying, "You dare not stop me." Konsuo paddled as fast as he could, but before he reached the center of the river, things changed. Zephyr gave way to wild wind and thunderstorm; the river became rough, making the canoe almost uncontrollable. With an unquenchable exuberance, though, Konsuo managed to control his canoe until he crossed the five-mile-wide river.

Upon reaching the far shore after his hazardous journey, Konsuo was tired and thirsty. To quench his thirst, he took a drink of water that he had brought along with him. He drank the water so fast that it choked him to death.

The Palm-Oil Daughter

*H*elp *from the spirit world and
destruction due to overriding jealousy are the core elements
in "The Palm-Oil Daughter," told by Rose Jallah.*

The Palm-Oil Daughter

*O*nce upon a time, there lived a native chief named Momolu. Momolu had two wives, Koisay and Korpo. Koisay, who was a jealous woman, had two daughters but Korpo had none. Their husband, however, loved Korpo more than he loved Koisay. He did everything that he could think of to help his most beloved wife find some kind of medicine that would enable her to bear at least one child. This made Koisay angry because she wanted to be the only one with children. She tried to find any means possible to stop her rival from bearing a child.

As time went on, Korpo's chances of having a child decreased. Koisay then increased Korpo's sadness by forbidding her children to talk to Korpo. Poor Korpo was all by herself, with nobody to talk to except her husband when he came home at night. She cried all day.

One day Korpo happened to pass through a wood. In the center of the wood she saw a tin of palm oil. To her surprise, the tin of palm oil began to talk and it said, "Stop crying, mother. I know your problem and I have decided to change myself into a beautiful little girl for you. But there is one condition. You have to promise that you won't reveal my story to anyone. If you do, you might cause sadness in your family." Korpo willingly consented to this condition and took her treasure home. When they reached their hometown, everybody came out to congratulate Korpo on her beautiful daughter. This palm-oil child was now the most beautiful girl in this village.

Koisay, being so envious, wanted to know how Korpo got her daughter. When it was time for Korpo to go to bed with their husband, the envious Koisay hid herself under their bed just to hear what Korpo had to tell her husband about her new daughter.

Finally, one night Momolu, who loved Korpo dearly, asked her how she got a child. Korpo, thinking that nobody else was around, then revealed her daughter's history. Koisay, having overhead the story, immediately went back to her hut and killed her two daughters so that she could get a beautiful palm-oil daughter too. Then she traveled from wood to wood, from forest to forest, but she never found a tin of palm oil. She began to regret killing her ugly children, who had at least kept her company. Now she who had had two children before had none because of her jealousy. Although Korpo and the rest of the family were sad because the poor children had been killed, Korpo and her daughter lived happily.

The moral of this story is that one should not be envious of what someone else has. We should be content with what we have. This moral is applicable even today. Some people are never content with what they have.

The Untrustworthy Girl

L I B E R I A

*L*offa County in northeast
Liberia is the home of the Loma people. A friend told Francis
Sei Korkpor this Loma story of the destruction of Hawa,
which illustrates the combined themes of greed and a lack of
faith.

The Untrustworthy Girl

*F*ar in the northern part of Loffa County there was a tiny river that ran between two villages. One of the villages, known as the Holy Village, had only two inhabitants—an old man and his wife in their late nineties. The population of the other village was composed of people whose ancestors were believed to have been transformed from fish from the tiny river into human beings. Where the river ran by the second village, it was known for all sorts of magical, supernatural powers. An evil-doer, for example, could not cross the river to and fro without drowning, despite its shallowness.

Most of the men and women in the second village lived decent lives, since crossing the river meant not only purity from sin but also the gaining of fame and glory from visiting the Holy Village across from it. Indeed, young people were not permitted to marry unless they had successfully crossed the river.

One day two girls from the second village decided to fulfill their obligation by crossing the river. Since the girls had not proved their fitness to live in the village by crossing the river, the other villagers treated them as dependent, irresponsible, and worthless, and the girls were tired of this. Hawa and Fatu, as the girls were called, left the village one foggy December morning and went to the river. As was the custom, the girls prayed to the river and promised to do whatever the old people in the Holy Village asked them to do so that they could obtain their reward and return safely to their people.

Stepping into the water for the very first time, the girls, who were pure from sin, found that their ankles were not even wet. They crossed the river easily and soon found themselves in the very quiet Holy Village, which was surrounded by a large banana bush. There was only one hut in the village. High grass grew halfway up the hut's walls, because it had been a long time since someone had visited and cut the grass. When they reached the village, Hawa's expression changed, for she had expected a very clean place with lively people. Fatu led the way along the winding path to the old hut, followed reluctantly by her disappointed friend. They saw two gray-haired old people, who were quite happy to see them.

After sitting and talking for a while, Fatu asked her friend to join her in cleaning around the old hut and bringing water for the old people. "Let me rest, yah," was Hawa's reply. Fatu began the work and Hawa unwillingly joined her, but only after the work was nearly done. Later, the old woman asked the girls to beat rice and cook it. Hawa murmured to her friend that she did not want to cook in the dishes, which were dirty. In fact, she refused to eat for the two days that they spent in the Holy Village, in order to avoid becoming sick.

The second and final day of the girls' stay at the Holy Village came. Toward noon the old people called the girls, thanked them, and gave each a certain amount of gold tied in a white handkerchief. The girls were strongly advised not to untie the handkerchiefs until they had crossed back over the river. Furthermore, the old man from the Holy Village was to escort them as far as the river. He would then transform himself into an alligator and carry each girl across the river, but they were warned again that the secret of the handkerchiefs must not be revealed. The girls were happy as they left for home.

While they were on the way down to the river, Hawa, who was very eager to know the amount of gold that she possessed, told Fatu and the old man to wait for her because she had to attend to nature. She went into the bush and untied the handkerchief. She was surprised by the huge amount of gold it contained. She quickly retied the handkerchief and hurried to the road, where she joined the other two.

When they reached the magic river, the girls lost sight of the old man. On the other side of the river the girls' parents, friends, and relatives had come to await them. Hawa saw them and waved happily to her people. Soon an alligator appeared on the surface of the shallow river.

Fatu jumped on the back of the alligator. It carried her up and down the river, testing her faith. Finally, she was carried ashore on the other side.

Now it was Hawa's turn; she jumped on the back of the animal. She became afraid and started trembling. She tried to hold fast to the alligator's tail as the beast carried her up and down the river. Finally, she could not stand the pressure any longer. She shouted in a loud voice, "What is this old man trying to do?"

When it heard this question, the alligator submerged and neither it nor Hawa was ever seen again. Hawa's own untrustworthiness caused her not to trust others, which brought about her own destruction.

The Canoe Man of West Point

*W*est Point is a peninsula jutting out into the Atlantic Ocean at the mouth of the Mesurado River on the north side of Monrovia, the capital of Liberia. The waters are very deep along this coast, and they are filled with extremely large fish. A. Golafale Shannon's story about Joe Blacks, a member of the Kru tribe who was known as "the canoe man of West Point," is set in this locale. In some respects the tale is reminiscent of Herman Melville's great American novel, Moby Dick.

The Canoe Man of West Point

*O*nce upon a time, there lived a canoe man in West Point called Joe Blacks. Everywhere he went he was loved and considered a man of honor. Joe Blacks was called upon for aid whenever there was a shortage of fish around the city of West Point. "Proud, indeed, I am, for my name is known all over the city as a courageous man of the sea who can help his people when they are in need," said Mr. Blacks.

One day Mr. Blacks called his mates to go out to sea to catch some fish to feed his community. That day was a day of sorrow, a day of sadness in the history of the fishermen of West Point, who looked to the sea for their livelihood. The tide from the sea was vexed because it could not find its wife; the fish were hungry because of the tide's condition. Nobody cared to go out to sea because the day was not conducive to fishing. However, there was a group of people who wanted to eat fish at their evening meal, so they started singing praise songs about Joe Blacks. "He-la-ma-la," they sang, meaning that Joe was the "man of his time and the ruler of the group." Joe became excited by the cheering crowd and called upon his men to go out to sea to catch some fish.

Looking at the blue sea for some minutes, he called his medicine's name three times—"ma-ma-ma," which means "spirit, of spirit." When they began moving on the water, it seemed that the canoe was trying to say something to him, and to his group indirectly, but its meaning could not be understood. Joe and his men rowed on out to sea, while the canoe seemed unhappy.

The day of disappointment had finally arrived, when far below the ocean's surface a hungry fish saw the yellow canoe breaking through the waves. Joe saw the fish and halted for some time, waiting for it to come closer. Meanwhile, the fish waited for Joe and his men. Suddenly, Joe began to paddle the canoe with terrific speed in order to get near enough to spear the fish, which was so huge that it could only be compared with an elephant.

Joe threw his spear, but it broke, and the elephant-fish, as it was called, was so mad that it rushed at the canoe with such force that it caused the boat to turn over. When the fishermen landed in the water, the only person that the fish attacked was Mr. Blacks. Joe, who had no faith in God, fought the elephant-fish, but the fish bit his arm off.

Some other fishermen from West Point found Mr. Blacks lying on the rocks, and they helped bring him home. He was taken to the hospital, where he spent two months recovering from an operation in which the doctor replaced his missing arm with an artificial one. When he returned home from the hospital, Joe decided to go back to sea to kill the elephant-fish that had wounded him. He gathered a crew to go along to kill the fish. As he prepared his new spears, he praised the devil, saying "In the name of the devil, I must kill that fish."

This second time he was successful in killing the elephant-fish. From that time on Mr. Joe Blacks was even more highly respected in his West Point community.

The Creek that Led to a New World

LIBERIA

*I*saac B. Rue was responsible for recording the tale "The Creek that Led to a New World," which is about how the inhabitants of an isolated Liberian village were introduced to a new world.

The Creek that Led to a New World

There was once a village that had very few families. All of the villagers thought that they were the only people who existed. The people of the village did not travel at all. They felt that they were created to stay within the vicinity of the village, and they did all that they could to remain near the village. In fact, the hunters were the only ones who ventured very far from the village.

One day a hunter who left the village could not find his way back home when evening came. His fellow villagers looked for him but they could not find him. At last they came to the conclusion that he was eaten by the evil spirits of the forest.

Meanwhile, the hunter did everything that he knew to do to try to return home, but he could not find the way back. As he wandered about in the forest, he ate wild fruits and slept under big trees. One morning soon after he got up and embarked on his search, he came to a creek. As he drank some water from the creek, he decided that he would stop moving all around in the forest, and instead he would follow the path of the creek. The hunter walked along the side of the creek for a week. On the eighth day of his journey he came to a strange village. The village was unknown to the hunter, but its people were very kind to him. After he told them how he had become lost, they helped him locate his own village.

When he got to his home village, his fellow villagers were so happy to see him again that they held a big feast for him. He told them just what had happened. They all became interested in this newfound outside world, and they decided to establish a relationship with the other villagers. From that time on, they no longer lived an isolated life. It was the hunter's accidental finding of the creek that caused the villagers who were living an isolated life to get to know the other villagers and the world beyond.

How a Proud Girl Perished

L I B E R I A

*T*he rescue of a beautiful girl from a Liberian river devil is the basic plot of "How a Proud Girl Perished," Euphania Abdullai's selection. The story-teller comments, "The good side of the story is that even though he knew Musu did not love him, Kiafa was willing to take her message home—that and the fact that Musu finally agreed to marry Kiafa. The bad side of the story is that Kiafa later insisted that the girl recite the words that made her disappear, maybe to return to the devil."

How a Proud Girl Perished

*O*nce there lived in a little village a beautiful girl named Musu. Because of her overweening pride in her beauty, Musu would not agree to marry any man. In this village there was also a young man whose name was Kiafa. Musu developed a kind of hatred for this man.

The village in which this girl lived was built on the bank of a river. In the river there lived a devil whose desire was to have a girl offered to him. All of the elders of the town got together and decided to offer Musu. When her parents found out what the townspeople's plans were, they advised the girl not to go anywhere out of the town, not even to the farm that the family cultivated on the other side of the river.[1] They warned her strongly to remain in their home.

One morning when her parents were leaving to go to work on their farm, Musu insisted on going too. She thought that the devil had forgotten about her. Her parents did everything that they could to persuade her not to go, but they failed and she went with them. That evening, when the day's work was over, they started back to the village in a thin dugout canoe. When the canoers reached the middle of the river, the current was very strong, and it carried them to a big rock where the devil lived. When they reached this rock, the canoe capsized. Everyone was saved except Musu. She disappeared. Searches were made for Musu, but she could not be found. Her relatives and friends mourned for her.

Kiafa, the man whom Musu hated, went to cut bamboo thatch in the swamp near the river where the devil's rock was situated. As he was about to cut the bamboo, Musu came out of the water and sat on the big rock. When she saw Kiafa, she asked him who he was. Kiafa plainly replied to her that he was the man whom she hated in the village. Musu told Kiafa to tell her parents to offer a sacrifice to

---

1. Rather than live on their farm, West African farmers often tend small areas of land outside the town in which they reside.

the devil. The sacrifice was a white chicken, two new sticks, and a pot of palm-oil rice. These were to be taken to the river so that the devil would release her, since she could not leave the rock on her own.

Kiafa left Musu on the rock and went back to the town to tell her parents what he had seen and heard. When Musu's parents heard the news, they were very happy, and they quickly went to an old lady who was a witch doctor. She told them to rub okra and soap leaves on the rock, so that when they went to see Musu she could slip off the rock. Her parents did as the witch doctor told them. Kiafa went back to the river and began cutting bamboo again; suddenly Musu came out of the water and sat on the rock. While talking to him she slipped off the rock. Kiafa caught her and carried her back to the town. Her parents were too too happy.[2] They immediately married her to Kiafa because he had rescued her. She gladly accepted Kiafa and they lived together for some time.

After ten years Musu's husband asked her to tell him what she had said when she was with the devil. She refused, but Kiafa insisted that Musu, being a woman and his wife, should obey him. Musu did as her husband wished. When she told him what she had said to the devil, she vanished and was never seen again.

---

2. *Too too,* extremely (used for emphasis).

The Poor Gentleman Who Lived among the Nobility

LIBERIA

"*The Poor Gentleman Who Lived among the Nobility" was contributed by Randolph B. Fahnubulleh.*

The Poor Gentleman Who Lived among the Nobility

Section I

There lived a very poor but very handsome fellow in a city filled with nobles. The young man was called Baranda. To the north of the city lay a large river with a beautiful sand bottom. In this city there also lived the richest king in the world. This king was called Munsa. He had eight children and four wives. His first child was named Ali. Three miles away from the city the most beautiful and poorest lady lived in a cabin; she was named Kolen.

The poor young man, Baranda, was a lover of water, as was the king's first child, Ali. Every afternoon both Baranda and Ali visited the riverside, sometimes to bathe, sometimes to look at the beautiful sandy bottom of the river. Notwithstanding their many simultaneous visits, these two young men were not acquainted with each other; they never spoke with one another. Each time they went to the riverside, any young women who passed by fell in love with Baranda simply because of his handsome appearance. The king's son became very envious of Baranda.

One afternoon, when the poor young man and the king's son were at the riverside and spoke with one another for the first time, they saw Kolen approaching them from the northeastern side of the river. The two men were both taken with her great beauty. When she reached where they were sitting, Ali asked her, "Where are you coming from?"

"From the northeast, my lord," she responded, "from a little cabin three miles away from here."

Ali then asked, "Is that where your parents live?"

"No," replied Kolen, "my parents are dead."

Ali said to her, "Come along with me into my father's palace, and I will give you food to eat and a place to rest." Poor Baranda did not utter a word.

The beautiful young woman went along with Ali into the palace, leaving Baranda alone at the riverside. Later the poor fellow heard a huge voice calling from under the water, "Baranda, Baranda, what is worrying you at the moment? Come closer to the river and you will see my wonderful performance." Baranda went closer to the river. When he looked at the bottom where only the white, sandy spot should have been seen, he saw both gold and diamonds scattered there. The poor fellow once again heard the voice: "Baranda, this talk between us should be confidential. Go and I will give you all that you need to know."

In the meantime, despite all of the riches that Kolen saw at the palace, she did not care for any; her thoughts were focused only on Baranda. After a month in the palace, she and Ali were in deep conversation when she asked him, "Where is your friend that I met with you at the riverside?"

He said to her, "I do not know the whereabouts of a poor man, and no poor man is a friend of mine." Kolen's feelings were hurt, since she too was poor, but she did not let Ali know her reaction to his statements.

One Sunday, Kolen asked Ali to walk with her to the riverside. When they got there they saw Baranda sitting by himself. They sat down opposite him. The lady asked, "Ali, who is that gentleman? Let him come and join our company."

Ali said, "That is the poorest fellow in the empire, and my father does not love a poor man, nor do I. Why should such a poor and dirty man keep company with you?"

Kolen said to Ali, "When my parents were dying, they told me that my future husband would be a poor man, not a rich one. Therefore, I love that poor and dirty man. I am poor too; my parents never owned a spoon to eat with, much less a palace. I would love living in the cabin with one that is poor like myself."

Ali said, "Baby, my father loves you, and he is not opposed to a poor, beautiful lady who would like to marry me. You are poor, but I can make you rich in a minute with my father's gold and diamonds."

Baranda left the riverside and returned to the city. Kolen left Ali and went toward the northeast, from whence she had come. Ali went to the palace and told his father that Kolen had said that she loved only Baranda, a poor man, and needed no riches. The king became very angry and sent for Baranda. When the young man was brought before him, the king said, "You prevented Kolen from marrying my son. Therefore, you will be put in jail for twenty-five years."

Section 2

One day when Baranda was in jail, the king's youngest daughter asked her father, "Papa, why did you imprison that innocent fellow?"

Munsa said to his daughter, "He prevented your brother from marrying Kolen, his chosen girl."

During his imprisonment, young women from all over the empire visited the jail to see Baranda, and each one fell in love with him. Hence, he gained wild popularity because of his handsomeness.

Innocently, Kolen visited the city one day to look for Baranda, not knowing that he had been jailed. She walked all around the city, but she could not find him. She then went to the riverside, where she met another rich fellow bathing. Kolen asked him, "My lord, do you know the most handsome and poorest young man who lives in this city?"

The man said, "Yes, Baranda is his name, and he was put in jail by the king of this empire." Then he said, "Why should you ask for a dirty fellow of this type, who has got nothing to give you? He is a criminal who stole from the king's palace. Come along and I will carry you to my father's mansion, and there you will live as long as you want to." Kolen refused to go with the young man. Instead, she returned to her little cabin in the northeast.

The rich young man ran to the palace and informed Munsa that Kolen had come to look for Baranda. He said she had now gone back to the northeast. The king got mad and passed a law that no one—be it girl, woman, man, or boy—should visit the jailhouse anymore. Anyone caught there would face capital punishment.

After Baranda had been in jail for three years, Munsa's youngest daughter visited him. She, too, fell in love with him. Unknown to her father, she started visiting the jailhouse regularly. One day she was caught there by Ali. Ali ran to the palace and told their father, "Papa, your daughter is with Baranda in the jail."

Once again the king got mad. He sent for his daughter. "I have passed a law that no one should visit the jail," he told her. "Why did you go there?"

She answered, "I love Baranda. Therefore, I visited the jail to meet him. If you do not release him, I will be his partner in the jail." Munsa ordered his generals to release the young man.

After Baranda left jail, he decided to look for Kolen. Munsa's daughter was deeply in love with him, but Baranda had never really loved her. He had simply consented to be with her because he wanted to be set free. So, the young man then went to look for Kolen. Unfortunately, he couldn't find her cabin because he went thirty-five miles to the northwest instead of the three miles to the northeast. He decided to return home. When he got to the city, he visited the riverside, and there he found the king's youngest daughter crying.

Baranda asked her, "Why are you crying?"

She responded, "For the dignity of love, dear. My love for you is too great. If you leave me, I will surely die."

The poor fellow said to the king's daughter, "I suppose I love you, but my parents told me a few years ago that I should not marry any rich lady. I cannot go against my parents' will; it is the only advice that they ever gave me. Therefore, I am very sorry because there is no possibility that I can marry you." Baranda left the king's daughter and went back to the city.

The daughter left the waterside, and before she could reach home she got seriously ill with a broken heart. Munsa sent for all of the doctors in the empire to come and care for her. She remained ill. The king became very worried. One Monday morning, the daughter called the king and told him, "I am dying for the love of Baranda. If I can get him to love me again, then my sickness will surely be cured."

Munsa quickly sent his generals to look for Baranda throughout the empire and to bring him back to the palace as soon as possible. The generals ordered the soldiers to do as the king requested. They went all around their empire for three months, but they could not find Baranda. They did not know that Baranda had been in his little mud house for several months without stepping outside. He had been thinking about Kolen. The soldiers returned to the palace and told the king that Baranda could not be found in the empire. Munsa became very distraught, and he started to cry. He entered his daughter's room and told her that the soldiers could not find the poor fellow. It was not long before the daughter died.

Kolen was present during the funeral of the king's daughter, although the father and son did not recognize her. She simply had come back to fetch Baranda. Immediately after the funeral, Baranda left his room to visit the waterside. Ali saw him walking toward the river. He shouted to his father, "There goes Baranda!" The angry king ordered everyone who had gone to look for Baranda to be executed for lying. The army generals carried out the king's order; the soldiers were put in front of a firing squad.

While he was at the riverside, Baranda thought about how he could find Kolen. After a few hours, he saw her in a pure white dress coming toward him. The poor fellow got up to meet her with a cheerful smile. Suddenly, Baranda heard a voice calling from under the river, "You shall be banished from this empire if you marry Kolen." The couple decided to return to town.

On their way home, they were seen and admired by many. One old priest, a neighbor of Baranda's, saw him with the beautiful Kolen. The old priest started to wonder about how Baranda fell in love with such a lady. One day, when the two young people decided to get married, they asked the priest to perform their marriage ceremony.

The old priest did not resist. He knew that love is not motivated merely by riches. He took them to his residence to marry them, and he invited many dignitaries in the city to the wedding.

Poor Baranda became skeptical about what the priest had done. He asked the priest, "Why have you done all this for me, my old priest?" In response the priest said, "Baranda, you are a poor fellow, and you want to get married. The Lord has instructed me to marry those who are in love, whether they are rich or poor."

Immediately after the wedding, the priest gave the young couple a house to live in. One day while they were living in this house, a young servant of the king saw them. The servant ran to the palace and told Munsa, "Sir, Baranda and Kolen are now married and are living in one of the old priest's houses."

The king did not believe the servant, but he called three of his nobles to him and directed them to the priest's house to find out whether it was true that the two young people were married. When the three nobles approached the priest's house, they saw Baranda and Kolen sitting on a rock in the yard. They ran back to the king and said to him, "King, it is true they are married and are living in the priest's house." The king became aggravated and he called all of his generals to the palace. He instructed them to banish the young people because an act had been passed a few years earlier which decreed that no poor man or woman could get married in the empire. The generals went to the priest's house and carried out the king's command.

Section 3

When Baranda and Kolen left the city, they went to the riverside. While they were standing there, they saw a very beautiful boat made of gold and diamonds on the surface of the river in the northwest. The young people started toward the boat. As they were about to reach it, it disappeared.

Baranda and Kolen traveled for three years, three months, three weeks, three days, and three hours. At last they arrived at a forest. Near this forest was located a very large lake. In this forest no human being was visible, except the two travelers.

Baranda left Kolen at the lakeside and walked toward the northwest. As he walked, he found a rusty cutlass lying between two trees. He took it and went back to Kolen and said to her, "I have found a very rusty cutlass; I will use it to build our cabin." Baranda cleared the spot for the cabin. The following day, he started building the cabin.

During the time that he worked on building the house, the couple slept near the lake. One Friday evening, Baranda had a dream in which a princess appeared before him. She was standing in a mansion, dressed in a pure gold dress. The princess told Baranda, "You will become a very rich gentleman through my aid. Come to the lakeside every Friday morning and pray to this lake." The prayer that the dream princess told him to recite was: "Lord, I promise not to pray to another god but Thou, my maker and my salvation. Thou, as my only helper, I depend on for all my needs." The princess told him that after reciting this prayer, he could ask for anything that he needed.

The next morning Baranda told his wife about the dream. Kolen became afraid that something ominous might happen. However, the husband remembered the time when he had visited the riverside and had heard a voice calling, "Baranda, Baranda, what is your worry at the moment? Come closer to the river and you will see my wonderful performance." He remembered going closer and seeing the bottom of the river covered with scattered gold and diamonds. He also remembered hearing another voice saying, "Baranda, this talk between us should be confidential. Go and I will give you all that you need to know." And another Sunday afternoon, he remembered that it has said, "You shall be banished from this empire if you marry Kolen."

Upon the completion of the cabin, the couple moved into it. They slept on a little bamboo bed. One Friday morning, Baranda left to go hunting. Kolen left immediately for the lakeside. When she got there, she recited the prayer that the princess had taught her husband. After reciting the prayer, Kolen asked for the beautiful boat made of gold and diamonds that they had seen on the river. When she opened her eyes, she saw the beautiful boat coming toward her. She became very happy and ran back to the cabin to wait for her husband.

Baranda returned at 3:00 P.M. Kolen met him with a very cheerful smile. "I have performed your duty," she told her husband.

Baranda asked, "What duty is that?"

She said, "I visited the lake this morning, and I recited the prayer she taught you; later I asked for the boat that we saw at the river on our way to the forest." Baranda became very cheerful when he learned what had happened.

They decided to go for a ride on the boat every afternoon at 3:00 P.M. First they visited the southeast, thirty miles away from the forest. There they saw a very beautiful city, but they did not land there. Upon their return, they saw a magnificent ship sailing from the southwest to the southeast.

On another Friday morning, Baranda visited the lake and recited his prayer. The young man asked for a beautiful mansion made of gold and marble to be built near the cabin. Before he opened his eyes, the mansion was built. The husband and wife moved into the mansion right away. Anything that one could wish for was to be found in it.

Baranda and Kolen lived there happily for three years. During the fourth year, the lady became pregnant. Nine months later, she delivered twin boys. One of the twins was blind and the other was crippled. They named the blind twin Rona and the crippled one Lona. The twins lived in the mansion until they became adults.

Baranda visited the lake another Friday morning. He recited his prayer once again and asked for 340 miles of paved road to be built, running from the northeast to the northwest. He also asked for cars and servants. Immediately, everything appeared. Baranda ran home and told his wife about the new gifts from their god.

The family lived in their forest until they became very affluent. One afternoon the parents and their two children sailed to the northwest. Unexpectedly, they saw the very city from which they had been banished, but they did not land. Kolen told her children how she and Baranda had met, the difficulties that they had experienced before marrying, and lastly, how they had been sent away from the empire by King Munsa.

When they returned to the forest, the same ship appeared that they had seen during their visit in the southeast. This ship was for their lord's princess and was simply on the lake to guard them wherever they went, though they did not know this.

When Baranda and Kolen became old, they told the twins how they had gotten all of their riches. They advised their children to honor, respect, and be grateful to their god. If they did so, the parents said, Rona and Lona would receive anything that they needed after Baranda and Kolen died. "Do not be selfish to one another, but rather live like brothers," the parents warned.

Three months later Baranda and Kolen died. Only the servants and the brothers were left in the forest. After a while, Rona left for the lakeside on a Friday morning. He knelt down and recited the prayer that his parents had taught him. Then he asked for a bigger, more beautiful city to be built. Surprised, Lona and the servants saw this large and beautiful city suddenly appear. The servants, who knew nothing of the prayer and the munificent god, became afraid. They saw a different type of people wearing a different style of clothing. They all spoke the same language. As time went on, the city became very industrialized.

The question arose between the two brothers about who would rule this unique city. Rona and Lona conferred frequently to decide who was to become the ruler, but they never arrived at any conclusion. The city grew to a stage where it could not function properly without a leader. A few individuals from the city visited the brothers and said, "We have appeared before you today to ask you to give us a leader for our city." Nevertheless, no concrete decision was made.

Four months later, Lona said to his brother, "We are suffering simply because of our deformities. Because of our riches, the fellows in the city do not love us. If we lived among them, they would kill us; therefore, let us kill ourselves. We won't commit any sin; our god of the lake will pray for us. Remember, our parents said before their deaths that we should love and respect one another."

Rona did not disagree with his brother. Lona decided that they should go and drown themselves in the lake. They set the date for their death. In actuality, however, Lona, the crippled twin, intended to kill Rona and thus become the leader. Rona, the blind twin, was quite unaware of Lona's plan. The date set for their death was Sunday at 3:00 P.M. The night before they were to drown themselves, Rona dreamed about Lona's plan.

The following day Lona visited the lakeside. He took a very big rock and tied it on a string. He hid his heavy stone near the lake and went back home. The appointed hour arrived. Lona called his blind brother and said, "It is now time to go and perform our duty." Rona took his walking stick and went along with Lona to the lake. The walking stick had a special property: when it touched any living thing, that thing died.

When the brothers reached the lake, Lona said, "Brother, since I can see, let me be the first to jump into the lake, and you can follow." Lona took his heavy stone and threw it into the lake. It made a loud sound—"bon, bon, bon."

Rona said aloud: "I was told by my parents that before I jumped into this lake, I should strike my surroundings with my walking stick." He struck the tall grass about him, not knowing that Lona was hiding in the tall grass near the lake. When he got near to where Lona had hidden, Rona lifted his walking stick high. When Lona saw the dreaded stick, he shouted out, "Do not kill me, brother Rona. I am not dead."

Rona stopped. The crippled brother said, "My intention was simply to kill you, since you are blind, and become the leader of this city. I have betrayed you, Rona, but please forgive me. Think about our parents' advice."

The two brothers left the lake and went back to their mansion. They never told any of the servants what had happened. Rona said to Lona, "Since you can see, you should be the leader of the city. It will be a great benefit to us." Since that time, the two brothers have lived in peace and harmony.

This story simply teaches us that one can be born poor and yet become the richest individual on earth. Perhaps the reader can find additional lessons in the tale.

Menynue's Aid to a Lame Man and a Blind Man

L I B E R I A

*T*hat good can be the ultimate result of evil done to another is seen by John C. Kwiah as the lesson found in "Menynue's Aid to a Lame Man and a Blind Man." The story comes from the Glaro Clan in the Sarbo Chiefdom in Grand Gedeh County, Liberia.

Menynue's Aid to a Lame Man and a Blind Man

*T*here was a little village called Sala in Glaro. In this village there was a law that no one should steal from another member of the village. This law continued for a long time and things went quite well. Then one day, a woman lost her lappa.[1] Everyone was called to a meeting. At the meeting, a committee was set up to prepare an ordeal to determine who had taken the lappa. This ordeal consisted of placing palm seeds in very hot oil. Anyone who removed these palm seeds from the oil without being burned was said to be innocent.

Soon everybody in the village had undergone this ordeal and was found innocent except for the lame man and the blind man. These two were led to the ordeal pot. The blind man was excused because he could not see the ordeal pot. The lame man tried to remove the palm seeds from the hot oil, but he could not do so, and he was found guilty. Then the lame man confessed that he and the blind man had stolen the lappa. They were asked by the villagers to leave the village at once.

The lame man could not walk and the blind man could not see; how they could leave the village was the question that the two men had to answer for themselves. The lame man suggested that the blind man should take him on his shoulders and he, the lame man, would direct the blind man.

The two thieves left the village for an unknown destination. They went until they came to a river. They stopped there because they could not cross. They spent three days near the river. There was no food and no way to get food. The lame man told the blind man that he was going to kill himself. The blind man began to cry and asked the lame man not to commit suicide.

---

1. *Lappa,* two yards of fabric that a woman wraps around herself for a dress.

As they were talking, there came a fisherman with his canoe and fishing line. The two men said not a word while the fisherman was near them. The fisherman left his canoe on the riverbank and went away. When the fisherman departed, the lame man told the blind man about the canoe. They got into the canoe and went off. They rode the canoe to a waterfall. This waterfall was not a steep one, and it did not cause them any problem. Soon they stopped by a rock. They had no food, only water, so they decided to go on and try to catch some fish.

When they decided to stop and fish, the blind man dropped his line into the water. There was no sign of fish in the area. Just as they were about to go somewhere else to fish, they heard a voice that told them to try fishing where they were one more time. They were afraid, yet they decided to try again. This time when the blind man dropped his line into the water, he caught a very big fish.

"Oh, please do not kill me," said the fish, whose name was Menynue.

"We will kill you for food-o," said the lame man.

"You must save me or else your condition will become worse than it already is," replied Menynue. "I need your help; that is why I came here."

"What do you want us to do for you?"

"I want you to take me to the large river."

"Where is the large river?"

"It is two miles from here," said the fish. "If you help me, I will help you also."

Upon hearing this, the lame man and the blind man started their journey toward the large river. When they got there, the fish told them to stop. "I want you to drop me here," said the fish.

"You promised to help us too. Where is our help?"

"Blind man," said the fish, "put your hand under the canoe." The blind man put his hand under the canoe and pulled out an egg. "Now," said the fish, "take that egg to shore but throw it on shore before you get there."

The blind man threw the fish into the water and did as it had advised him. When the blind man threw the egg on shore, it landed with a great "bomp" that shook everything around. Upon hearing the sound, the blind man regained his sight and the lame man regained his strength. The spot turned to a big city before their eyes. Then they heard a voice saying, "That is your city; go and live there." Thus, the lame man and the blind man had their city and they lived there very happily for many years.

Now the question: were the villagers cruel or kind to the lame man and the blind man?

The Mammy Water

LIBERIA

*M*any families in the Americo-
Liberian community, especially those living in Monrovia,
can trace their line back to the settlers who arrived from the
United States and the Caribbean in the mid-nineteenth cen-
tury. Naturally, some of these people brought folktales with
them from their former homes. Donald Thompson Ekanen's
"The Mammy Water" is one such story, having originated
on the island of Grenada in the West Indies.

The Mammy Water

*M*ost parents on the island of Grenada tell their children this story so that it can be passed on to the next generation.

In riverine areas most of the water dwellers believe that there is a great city under the sea and that it is a place of much wealth. They also hold the view that this city is ruled by the Queen of the Sea, the mammy water. Now, the problem is how to get to this city and acquire the wealth therein. Since the average man cannot get there, most young men think that the best way to get there is to marry the queen of this great empire.

The mammy water's abode is the sea, although she comes out on the land occasionally. She is said to be very beautiful with fair skin and dark, curly hair. She is always well dressed in immaculate white apparel. From the breast up she is human; below she is a fish. Apart from being the queen of the underwater dominion, she also has control over all of the creatures under the sea, whether big or small.

The beautiful woman comes out of the ocean every once in a while and sits by the mouth of a stream to adorn herself. She comes out very late at night, when people are not likely to be around to see her. However, it is during this particular time that some brave young men hide in hopes of seeing her. She adores handsome and fair-skinned young men, so she may appear to them. At their first sight of her, the men may be very fearful because of the charm that she possesses. She hypnotizes them and then asks them for their request. The dialogue ends with a request for marriage. When both parties have come to a mutual agreement, a slow wave carries the two of them under the sea. In the company of the queen the man is safe from any accident under the water.

Under the sea the man's head is turned the other way 'round like those of many undersea creatures who live in the mammy water. His face is turned to his back and the back of his head faces the front part of his body. Then a big party is held with lots of pomp and pageantry. Sea creatures from far distant areas are invited, and there is always much merriment. Some fishermen have said that at times they hear the sound of music from certain parts of the sea as they go about fishing. Some have even reported seeing structures that look like houses under the sea when they go deep diving. These men claim that they have certain powers to observe these things that cannot be seen by ordinary men.

It is said that a man can remain with the mammy water for some time and then return to land. He could be a bachelor or a married man on land—it makes no difference to the queen. Under this arrangement, the man can pay occasional visits to the queen while maintaining his relationship with his family on land. However, at a stipulated time he is finally required to return to the sea or bear the consequences.

Before he leaves the queen after the marriage ceremony, the man is given certain powers. With these powers he can change into any sea animal, and he can travel underwater for any distance without any harm. Hence, he could then turn into a crocodile, shark, whale, or any of the big sea creatures.

On returning to the land he becomes a very rich man. Any business that he undertakes will be successful. He has lovely and beautiful children from his wife on land, but these children do not live long because the queen may use them.

In order to maintain a good relationship with the queen, the man must perform yearly human sacrifices to her. For his wealth to continue to increase, this has to be done.

The man can accomplish this task in various ways. Since he has been given the power to change into any of the sea animals, he can utilize this means to wreck boats, ships, and steam engines. He can also capture innocent bathers by the beach. Most of the time when we hear about shipwrecks and high-sea disasters, this may be the cause. People caught this way are hypnotized and carried to the queen alive. They serve as workers and maids, and some carry money to the queen's man on land.

We are told that most of the men who are involved in this kind of life are extremely rich, and they can afford to build luxurious executive mansions. Some of the richest men in the West Indies are involved in this type of life. They run most of the big businesses and employ many workers.

Storyteller's commentary: The evil in this story is the killing of human beings by the man. He causes a great loss in human lives. Many innocent people have been killed due to greed. The man even goes so far as using his own children for sacrifices when he cannot get anyone else. Most of the queen's men misuse the powers given them and thus attack persons whom they hate and thereby destroy them. This method of gaining wealth is very unnatural and evil.

The only good part I see in this tale is that some of the men involved actually make good use of their powers. They help in the construction of bridges across certain troublesome waters by appealing to the queen of that particular water. Money and wealth gotten from the queen are used for the benefit of others, most especially the underprivileged. The men own large businesses whereby they can employ the jobless and also manufacture the basic things needed by common people.

However, parents warn their children and tell them this story so that they can avoid this kind of life since these men never end well. They finally return to the sea and what becomes of them nobody can tell.

The Result of Wickedness

*P*eople have emigrated to Liberia from countries other than the Americas and the Caribbean, of course. When Dorothy D. Chieh's grandparents traveled to Liberia from Nigeria, they carried with them the following tale of kindness and jealousy.

The Result of Wickedness

*O*nce upon a time, there was a hunter named Kulu who had two wives. The wives were named Tuwlo and Tanneh. Tuwlo was the head wife, and Tanneh was the junior wife. Tuwlo, being the head wife, was very arrogant, and she despised the junior wife, who was more beautiful than she.

Every day Kulu abused his wives because they had not borne any children after twelve months of marriage. But fortunately, Tuwlo became pregnant and bore a girl who was named Putu. Several months later Tanneh gave birth to a fine baby boy. There was great rejoicing for Kulu, for he had prayed very hard for a male child. The boy child was named Kulupo. Kulu was a very happy man.

When Kulupo was five years of age, Kulu took him along on his hunting trips. He began showing his son all kinds of little tricks pertaining to hunting, and when they reached home, Kulu told Tanneh all of the tricks that their son had learned and how clever he was. All of these daily occurrences made Tuwlo even more jealous of Tanneh and her son; she could no longer stand Kulu's favoritism for Tanneh.

One day Tuwlo went to a witchdoctor, from whom she got some poison. When she got home, she mixed some of the poison with Tanneh's food. Tanneh ate the food and became very sick. Kulu went to all the native doctors in their village, but none could save Tanneh's life. Kulu mourned deeply at the death of his wife, but whenever Kulu saw Kulupo he became consoled, for Kulupo resembled his mother greatly. After some months Kulu got over the death of his wife and began his hunting trips again.

Every time Kulu went hunting, Tuwlo beat Kulupo and gave him all of the hard work to do. She warned Kulupo not to mention any of this to Kulu. Tuwlo even made Putu hate Kulupo.

One day while Kulu was hunting, Tuwlo gave Kulupo a basinful of dirty dishes and three spoons to wash at a nearby river. As Kulupo was washing, he began singing. Accidentally, he dropped one of the spoons into the water, and it went straight down to the bottom of the river. Kulupo ran home crying and told Tuwlo what had happened. Tuwlo beat him and told him not to come back home until he had found the spoon. Kulupo went back to the river crying. When Kulupo reached the river he saw an old lady, who asked what was the matter. Kulupo told her about his trouble. The old lady told him to swim down to the bottom of the river. There he would find some people and he should do whatever they asked him to do. Kulupo was encouraged by the old lady's advice, and he dived down to the bottom of the river.

As Kulupo reached the bottom, he saw an old man bathing. The old man was trying to scrub his back. When he saw Kulupo, he begged him to help, which Kulupo did. Next, as Kulupo went on, he saw an old lady covered with sores. She asked Kulupo to help her bandage her sores; again, Kulupo did not refuse. After Kulupo finished, the old lady thanked him. She told him to go to a small flower garden, where he would see some flowers with buds. Some would be noisy and some would be quiet. She told him that if he picked three of the quiet buds and took them home before opening them, he would get what he was looking for. Kulupo thanked the old woman and went home with the three quiet buds.

When Kulupo got home, he avoided Tuwlo and Putu and went to his room. He closed the door and window and broke open the first bud. To his surprise he found in it spoons of different sizes and qualities, including Tuwlo's missing spoon. He opened the second bud; there he found gold, diamonds, silver, clothes, and shoes. Then he opened the last bud. In it he founds bags of money, more jewelry, and all kinds of hardware. Kulupo was very happy. He divided his riches into three portions. He gave one-third of his riches to Tuwlo and her daughter and told them about his experience. When Kulu came home from hunting, he was quite happy with the riches that were waiting for him.

Early the next day, the jealous Tuwlo, not satisfied with what Kulupo had given her, sent her daughter, Putu, to the river to wash a basinful of dirty dishes with three spoons. Tuwlo instructed Putu to purposely drop a spoon in the river in the same manner as

Kulupo had. Putu did as her mother told her. After dropping the spoon into the river, she started crying. Then she saw the old lady who had helped Kulupo. The woman asked her what was the matter. Putu related her story to the lady. The old woman told her to dive down to the bottom of the river, where she would see some people. Putu was instructed to do exactly whatever they asked her to do. Putu immediately dived down to the bottom. She first met the old man who was bathing. Again he was trying to scrub his back, but when he saw Putu he begged her to help him. Putu refused. Next, Putu met the old woman with the sores, who asked Putu to help her tie her bandages, but Putu said that she could not bear the smell of the sores. Therefore, she would not help bandage them. The old lady did not pay attention to what Putu said, but told the girl to go to the little garden and to pick three quiet buds so that Putu could get what she was looking for. Stubborn Putu went to the garden and picked three *noisy* buds, thinking that the old lady had tried to fool her.

When Putu got home, she went to her room and closed her door and window. She didn't wait to burst the buds one at a time, but instead she broke open all three at once. To her horror she found snakes, mosquitoes, termites, bees, wasps, and flies that all attacked her. Putu began to scream for help; when her mother went to her rescue, Tuwlo also was attacked by these creatures.

The Man Who Struggled to Survive

*A*len Damiano A. Buolo's "The
Man Who Struggled to Survive" is another example of a tale
that originated in a culture outside West Africa and is transmitted by members of a minority community now living in
West Africa. In this case religion is a contributing factor, as
the story is of Muslim derivation.

The Man Who Struggled to Survive

*T*his story took place in the Mediterranean Sea between 1900 and 1915. A ship crossing the sea from Egypt to Spain had among its passengers the three compatriots Hassan Mubark, Sherffadyn Yusif, and Mirray Ling. They were all Egyptians, but the first two were close acquaintances from the same area in Egypt. Mubark and Yusif were Muslims; Ling was a pagan. All of them were going to Spain on different missions.

When they went on board the ship, the three countrymen were lodged in two adjacent cabins—the two Muslims were in the same cabin and the pagan was in another one with someone else. Ling soon found out that Yusif and Mubark were from the same country as he was, so a few minutes after the ship left the port of Alexandria, he went to their cabin to visit them. He introduced himself to them, and they began chatting about various topics. After lunch, Ling came back to the two friends to continue their chat. There was a short silence that was interrupted by Ling asking, "Friends and countrymen, since you are Muslims, I hope you will satisfy my curiosity. Can either of you tell me the imperative reason that makes every faithful Muslim pray five times a day?"

"The Koran, our holy book, instructs us to do so," answered Mubark.

"Why does the Koran say so?" continued Ling.

"The Koran is a holy book, and we as Muslims must obey its teachings, no matter what reason it gives for doing so," replied Yusif. This answer did not convince Ling. He had cards in his pocket; he told the others that they should play a game for money. Ling took out ten Egyptian pound notes and put them on the table. Yusif and Mubark took out fifteen pound notes each. Ling knew how to play cards very well; the two Muslims did not know how to play as well as he did. Once they began playing, it did not take long for Ling to win the thirty pounds from the two friends.

After a short pause, Yusif declared, "As an honest Muslim, I am not supposed to have played this dirty game. I don't understand it, either."

"Does your religious law say that whenever you don't know something you shouldn't say so? Why did you not tell me that you do not know how to play cards?"

"Why do you ask me this question in that manner and what do you mean by referring to our religion contemptuously?"

"I referred to your religion because you quoted it as a basis for your not having played this 'dirty game.'" replied Ling, walking out the door.

Yusif became angry. He complained to Mubark that they had been cheated and that they should regain their money by any means. Mubark tried to convince Yusif that they were to blame for having agreed to play the game, but Yusif still insisted that they had been cheated. He said to Mubark, "Did you not observe the way this pagan mixed the cards? He did it so fast that you could hardly realize the trick he was playing. We have to claim back our money, anyway." Mubark looked confused.

Yusif went to Ling's cabin followed by Mubark, but they could not find Ling there. Yusif and Mubark climbed on the deck and looked around for Ling; they saw him sitting on top of the last cabin. They quickly walked toward him.

"Will you return our money that you took by deceit?" barked Yusif at Ling.

"I have no money for you. Please get away from me," replied Ling.

Before Ling could complete his last word, Yusif pushed him. He fell into the sea and he disappeared under the water for a few seconds; then he reappeared. The two friends murmured some curse words in Arabic and ran away from the scene. They decided not to say anything about the incident.

Meanwhile, Ling was struggling in the water. He swam for about a half an hour. The ship was now too far away for Ling to catch up with it. In fact, the ship was so far away that the people on board would not have been able to see a person in the water from such a distance. He kept on swimming until he was exhausted. He looked around for any sign of a ship; he did not see anything except for a round object floating toward him some fifty yards away. This gave him hope; he collected the little energy that he had left and swam toward the object. It was shaped like a lifebuoy, but it was made of grass bundled together and wound around with an elastic string. It was about three feet in diameter and one foot thick. He caught it and hung onto it, breathing heavily. However, Ling's troubles were not over.

Ling saw a sudden surge just in front of him, inside the ring. He could not believe his eyes! A big gray snake stuck its head out of the water and looked in the direction that Ling was floating. Ling thought quickly; he drew his head below the water, leaving only his nose sticking out so that he could breathe, while he still hung on to the ring. Ling wanted to abandon the ring, but he remembered the fatigue that he had experienced. He also remembered that he had a pen knife in his pocket. Ling decided that he could defend himself from the reptile with this weapon, if he was attacked—and he certainly did not intend to provoke the snake. However, the snake did not stay on the surface of the water for long. It went back under the water, and Ling quickly stuck his head back up.

The head of the snake came up again and immediately back down went Ling's head. Three times the snake came to the surface and then went down below the water. When the head of the snake sank for the third time, Ling was worried because he did not know how long the snake and he could continue this up-and-down movement without a crisis.

He looked around quickly; he saw a ship about five hundred meters away. The distance was still too far for him to swim. However, the urge to abandon this snake-possessed ringed object was growing. He thought that with rescue approaching, he should not act stupidly and lose his life, so he decided to wait until the ship was about half that distance from him. While swimming toward the ship, he collected all of his energy and shouted and waved. At last the ship responded. It slowed down and a boat with three members of the crew was sent after him. They picked him up and as soon as he was in the boat, he fell asleep.

Storyteller's commentary: This story portrays man's struggle against man and the indifference of nature to that survival. The two friends wanted to kill Mirray Ling. The sea, however, did not care whether the man saved himself. At the same time, the ringed object, which I would say had been brought around the man by chance, which in turn could be attributed to nature, helped to save Ling, though the snake beneath it could have finished him off.

Man is evil and good at the same time. Nature is indifferent, since it helps or destroys man haphazardly.

Crocodiles Shed Genuine Tears

*A*lex Attia, a Bassa man, ex-
plains that "Crocodiles Shed Genuine Tears" can be understood in terms of two Bassa sayings: "The same thing you do
to me, someone will do to you," which is fairly straightforward, and "The thing that is sweet in a small boy's mouth
will soon ruin his stomach," meaning that the very thing that
brings pleasure to a person will be his undoing if he continues to indulge in it.

Crocodiles Shed Genuine Tears

*O*nce upon a time in a village way back in the Liberian bush, there lived a very wicked old hunter. The main targets of his hunts were innocent children and helpless animals. Most of the time he had no real need to kill the animals, but hunting them had become a pleasant pastime for him. He got immense joy and satisfaction from seeing these animals struggle for survival against an unbeatable foe. He loved to see the looks on the faces of his victims as they writhed in deep pain. Indeed, this old hunter was truly cruel. He was an evil man. He was determined to show no mercy to weaklings, for his own crippled son had been killed in a fight by a more healthy boy. Ever since then, the old hunter showed no sympathy toward the helpless.

Now, not too far from the village, there flowed a muddy river. In that muddy river were the biggest and most vicious crocodiles one ever came across. These crocodiles lay in the river, waiting for any creature that dared enter the water.

The old hunter wanted to be really cruel to anything that was in any way helpless; still, try as he would, the hunter could never muster up enough courage to be as terrible as he wanted to be. In these crocodiles the old hunter saw the viciousness with which he wanted to dispose of his victims. He therefore fed the crocodiles with helpless animals daily. He especially enjoyed watching the crocodiles "shed tears" for their victims. He came each day with his victims, and the crocodiles came to anticipate his daily visits. He loved bringing helpless animals and the crocodiles enjoyed being fed. He brought rabbits, squirrels, and on special occasions—such as his birthday—be brought a helpless boy or girl to feed to the crocodiles. The crocodiles and the hunter became friends.

On one of these special occasions, the hunter went to the creek of another village and kidnapped one of the boys who had gone there to swim. He forcefully tore off the boy's undershirt and with it tightly gagged and tied up the innocent child. With his victim under his arm, he proceeded to the muddy river.

As he neared the river, he saw a baboon heading in the same direction. "Ah!" he thought, "Now I can have two shows instead of one-o." With this in mind, he cautiously followed the baboon. The baboon started drinking from the river. The hunter carefully put the boy down and started going slowly toward the baboon with the intention of pushing it into the river where the crocodiles were waiting. However, much to his surprise and great delight, one of the crocodiles suddenly leaped out and grabbed the baboon's hand. The baboon immediately gripped the trunk of a nearby tree. A violent tug-of-war ensued, the crocodile on one end strongly fighting for its meal and the baboon on the other end struggling for its very life with the tree trunk being its only hope for survival. When the old hunter saw that the baboon was gaining a better footing, he decided to cut the trunk. As soon as the hunter cut the trunk, the baboon grabbed the old man's foot and together they fell into the river.

Would you believe that before devouring the hunter the crocodiles shed genuine tears for the first time? Yes, they did. They shed real tears because the old hunter had been a major source of their food. He fed them every day, did he not? The crocodiles had to be fed today and surely one baboon was not enough. Since the hunter was there now, they had to eat what was available for them.

The Two Kings of Mali

M A L I

*I*n the eighteenth century the *Segou empire, which was located on the Niger River in central Mali, was ruled by a king named Da Monson. South of Segou was the kingdom of Samanyana. The ruler of this kingdom was named Samanyana Basi. "The Two Kings of Mali" is about a conflict between these two rulers, which is complicated by a soothsayer and a woman. The tale is part of an epic cycle about Da Monson that is told among the Bambara people.*

The Two Kings of Mali

*D*a Monson, the king of the Segou kingdom, was a very powerful man. He knew the secrets of all things that live—plants, animals, and people— and he was familiar with the wisdom known to the wisest of men of his time. Indeed, he was so famous for his power and wisdom that there was no one in the world who did not know his name.

Samanyana Basi was the ruler of the neighboring kingdom of Samanyana. He, too, was well-known, though he was neither as great nor as famous as Da Monson. Although he was a man of only average height, he had a perfect body. On his chin, highlighting his handsome face, he wore a small beard.

The Bambara people customarily enjoy drinking millet beer and honey wine together. One day, Samanyana Basi traveled to Segou to partake of the local liquor. Dressed in his most gorgeous robes of fine cloth and bright colors, he was a striking figure. When Da Monson saw his neighbor king, he realized that the man was even greater and more handsome than he had been told.

Grabbing hold of Samanyana Basi's beard, Da Monson greeted the visiting king: "Samanyana Basi, what a sweet, small beard you have."

Samanyana Basi replied coolly, "Why, my neighbor, do you not know why I wear this beard? Because of it I can see into the future."

For Da Monson this answer was an insult, a challenge to his own power. He immediately wanted to kill the other man on the spot, but he knew that the laws of hospitality prevented him from mistreating a guest. Instead, he quickly made plans to wage war on Samanyana Basi and to capture this boastful king.

No sooner had Samanyana Basi left to return home than Da Monson put his plans into practice. He sent his two best groups of warriors to attack Samanyana. In spite of the fact that these great warriors fought courageously, they were soundly defeated. When Da Monson learned of their failure, he grew both angry and ashamed at the defeat.

Da Monson was a stubborn man, however. In order to determine how best to defeat his enemy, he called together all of the wise men, soothsayers, and sorcerers to discover what could be done. Surely among these men, some of whom could see into the past and some of whom could see into the future, there would be one able to tell him how to accomplish his goal—to tell him what sacrifices needed to be made and what potions would be most helpful. While these men were on their way to Segou, Da Monson reviewed all that he knew about such matters. By the time the seers had gathered, he had devised a test for them. In a large, black, wooden bowl he hid a white rooster under a black cloth. When he was finished, he placed a turtle under a white calabash and covered the calabash with a white cloth.

To all of the assembled wise men Da Monson announced, "I want to find out who knows the purest of truth. If any of you can tell me what is under the black cloth and the white cloth, then I will know that you are a teller of the truth, and you shall be chosen to help me in my quest."

For many days the assembled wise men attempted to determine what was under the two cloths. No one was successful. Then an old soothsayer said to Da Monson, "That thing which is under the black cloth is covered by night. It is like white cloth with blood on it." Da Monson was amazed. The wooden bowl was certainly black like night, and the white rooster had a blood-red comb.

"That is right," said Da Monson.

Next the old man said, "The thing that is under the white cloth is covered by day. It is like a small stick with a lizard's head. It does not move and then it moves."

Da Monson was almost beside himself with happiness, for the white calabash was like day, and a turtle shell is hard like a stick and a turtle's head is like that of a lizard, and a turtle does not move and then it moves. He said to the old man excitedly. "You have told the truth. Now I want you to share with me the secret of how to defeat Samanyana and capture Samanyana Basi."

The old soothsayer said, "Samanyana can be destroyed and Samanyana Basi can be captured, but certain things must be done first to ensure that this will happen. You must obtain his first handful of food from his dinner, and his hat, and his sandals. Then we will devise a plan."

Da Monson called together his most trustworthy men and told them that they had to find someone who could obtain Samanyana Basi's first handful of food from his dinner, and his hat and sandals. For quite some time Da Monson's men tried to find someone who could do these things. Then one day a woman named Ten arrived in the town. She was the most beautiful woman ever to have walked on the earth. Any man who saw her would immediately fall in love with her. Ten was the daughter of a praise singer, and she knew the secrets of capturing a man's heart and destroying his mind.

Ten arrived at Da Monson's court and, kneeling before him, said, "I have come to declare myself your humble servant and to offer you whatever help I may be able to give."

"And what do you want in return for this great service?" asked Da Monson.

"I want the best that can be found in your treasury—jewelry of gold, silver, and precious stones, together with cowry shells and the finest cloth. Then I want your brewers to brew their best millet beer and honey wine. To this I will add a special medicine so that when a man drinks this liquor he will lose his ability to think and I will be able to control him."

As Ten instructed, the brewers brewed their best beer and wine. To this she added her secret medicine. Da Monson then gave Ten a canoe that was propelled by his four most capable canoe men, and she set forth on the Niger River to visit Samanyana. When the canoe reached its destination, the four paddlers drew it to the beach. For the next three days Ten sat in the canoe like a great queen, lying under a royal tapestry that was stretched over her to protect her from the sun.

At his court Samanyana Basi was told that a beautiful woman had arrived in a canoe, a woman so beautiful that none had ever been seen who was her equal. Samanyana Basi wondered about the woman. He was interested in finding out who she was, but he was fearful that she had been sent to do evil to him. Soon, though, his curiosity got the best of him, and he sent some of his entourage to bring her to him. As was the custom, when Ten appeared before Samanyana Basi, she was offered a gourd full of millet beer in greeting. Ten drank the beer in one gulp. Another gourd was offered to her, and she drank it in one gulp.

The people were astonished. "How is it that you can drink our best and strongest beer as if it were but water?" they asked.

"My goodness, was that your best beer?" Ten replied. "In Segou we give our children better beer than that to drink when they come in from play. We would hardly consider that a man's drink, let alone a drink to be drunk with your great king."

The people responded, "Ah, as our elders say, 'If a woman swallows a turtle, a man must swallow a lizard.'"

Samanyana Basi looked at the woman. "So, you think that Da Monson's beer is better than mine, do you?"

"I mean no disrespect, great king, but there is no comparison. Why, if you think this beer is strong, a single sip of Da Monson's beer will make you lose your mind."

Basi remained silent for a while. Finally, he said, "And how might I get some of this strong beer of which you speak?"

"Oh," replied Ten, "I have some of Da Monson's millet beer along with some honey wine in my canoe. I will be happy to send for some, if it please your highness."

Samanyana Basi sent his servants to the canoe, and they returned with the two large jugs, one filled with millet beer and one filled with honey wine. He quickly helped himself first to the beer, then to the honey wine. When he was finished, Ten knew that her trap had been sprung successfully. Thus it was that she managed to convince Samanyana Basi to have her servants and advisors leave them alone. She also convinced the king that she was a fine cook, and with his consent, she set about preparing their dinner.

When Samanyana Basi reached into the bowl to take his first handful of dinner, Ten pretended to bump into him accidentally and she knocked the food from his hand. The king was so smitten by Ten's beauty and so far under the influence of the doctored beer and wine that he hardly noticed what was going on about him. Ten scooped up the handful of food and wrapped it in a cloth. A few moments later the powerful medicine in the beer and wine took full hold of Samanyana Basi's senses, and he fell asleep. Ten jumped up, grabbed his hat and sandals, and slipped out of the house.

The canoe hurriedly returned Ten to Segou, where she delivered her captured treasures to Da Monson. Da Monson gave the handful of food, the hat, and the sandals to the old soothsayer, who shortly devised certain potions that would allow Da Monson's army to destroy Samanyana and capture Samanyana Basi. Because of this magic, the actual battle was quite short. Samanyana was destroyed, and Samanyana Basi was captured and beheaded on the spot.

Thus it was that by using her beauty and her knowledge, Ten destroyed one king and his kingdom and in turn increased the power of another king. It is said that a woman may be beautiful, but that she can be evil at the same time. As the elders say, "What is honey to one man may be poison to another."

The Creation of
the Universe

*F*or centuries Ife was the principal city of the Yoruba people. Located in the southwest corner of Nigeria, it was also a sacred city. "The Creation of the Universe" describes how the universe, Ife, and human beings were created.

The Creation of the Universe

*A*t the beginning of time the universe consisted only of the sky, the water, and marshland. Olorun, the most powerful and wisest of the gods, was the creator of the sun and the ruler of the sky. Olokun was the ruler of the waters and the marshes. Even though her kingdom contained no plants, animals, or human beings, Olokun was happy with it. Unfortunately, Obatala, one of Olorun's favorites, was not pleased.

"The world would certainly be more interesting if living things inhabited it," he said to Olorun. "What can we do so that Olokun's kingdom can be inhabited? What she needs is mountains, forests, and fields."

"Well," Olorun answered, "I agree that mountains, forests, and fields would be better than water alone, but how would it be created?"

"With your permission, I will create the solid land."

Olorun gladly gave Obatala permission to create the solid land. Obatala immediately went to see Orunmila, Olorun's oldest son, a god with the gift of being able to foresee the future.

"Olorun has given me permission to create solid land where now only water and marshland exist," he said to Orunmila. "Will you teach me how to do this so that I can then populate the world with living things?"

"I will be happy to, Obatala. You must first obtain a golden chain that is long enough to reach from the sky to the water. You must then take a snail's shell and fill it with sand. Next you must place the snail's shell, a white hen, a black cat, and a palm nut in a bag. When you have done this, you must carry them down to the marshland by way of the chain."

Obatala immediately went to find the goldsmith. The goldsmith agreed to make such a chain, but he did not have enough gold on hand to complete the task. So, Obatala went to all of the gods and asked them for the gold that they possessed so that the chain could be made. Because the gods agreed that Obatala's project was a worthy one, they gave him their golden necklaces, bracelets, and rings. Still, according to the goldsmith, Obatala had not collected enough gold to make a chain of sufficient length to reach from the sky to the water. He returned to the goldsmith anyway, and he asked the smith to fashion a chain as long as possible with what gold they had and to put a hook at the end of it.

When the chain was readied, Obatala and Orunmila hooked one end of it to the edge of the sky, and Orunmila gave Obatala the sand-filled snail shell, the white hen, the black cat, and the palm nut to put into a bag, which he slung over his shoulder. Obatala then began to climb down the golden chain.

When he had climbed down about half the length of the chain, Obatala realized that he was leaving the world of light and entering the world of twilight. Still he continued to climb down. When he reached the end of the chain, he was still far above the ocean, much too high to jump safely.

As he was wondering what to do, he heard Orunmila's voice call out from above. "Obatala," he said, "use the sand in your snail shell."

Obatala did as Orunmila dictated. He pulled the snail shell out of his bag and poured the sand into the water.

"Now free the white hen."

Obatala again obeyed Orunmila's command. The white hen fluttered down to land upon the sandy waters. She immediately began to scratch at the sand, scattering it far and wide. Wherever the grains of sand landed, dry land was created, the largest piles becoming hills.

Seeing the dry land grow high beneath him, Obatala let go of the golden chain and fell the short distance to the earth. The place where he landed he named Ife. He looked around and saw that the ground stretched as far as the horizon in every direction that he could see, but it was still barren.

Now Obatala dug a hole in the ground and buried the palm nut. He had barely shoveled the last handful of dirt over the nut when a palm tree began growing out of the buried nut. The tree quickly reached its full height and grew more palm nuts, which dropped upon the land and grew into mature trees before his eyes. Obatala took the bark from the trees and built a house. He gathered palm leaves and made a thatched roof for the house. When he went inside his new house, Obatala took the black cat out of the bag, and he settled down with the cat as his companion.

After some time, Olorun wondered how Obatala was doing, so he asked one of his servants, Chameleon, to go down the golden chain to visit Obatala. When the Chameleon saw Obatala, he said, "Olorun, the ruler of the sky, has asked me to find out how you are doing."

"Tell Olorun that the land and vegetation that I created are quite nice, but it is always twilight here and I miss the brightness of the sky world."

The Chameleon returned to Olorun and told him what Obatala had said. Olorun was so pleased with Obatala's effort that he said, "I will create the sun." He then did just that, and every day the sun's light and warmth poured down upon Obatala and his creations.

A great deal more time passed, and Obatala found that he was still not satisfied. "As much as I love my black cat," he said, "I think that I need another kind of companionship. Perhaps it will be good for me to populate this world with creatures more like myself."

Obatala set about to accomplish this task. He began digging in the soil, and he gathered together bits and pieces of clay that stuck together. Taking this clay, Obatala created small figures shaped like himself. This endeavor proved to be very tiring, and soon Obatala decided to take the juice from the palm trees to make palm wine. As tired as he was, he drank more of the wine than he realized, and soon he was drunk.

When Obatala began making the clay figures again, the effects of the wine made him a little clumsy. As a result, the figures that he created were not as well made as those that he had fashioned earlier. Some of the new figures had arms that were too short or legs of uneven length or a curved back, although Obatala's senses were so dulled from the drink that he did not notice that these figures were not perfect.

After he had created a large number of clay figures, Obatala called up to Olorun: "Olorun, I have created clay figures to populate my world and be companions to me, but they are devoid of life. Of all of the gods, you are the only one who can bestow life. I ask that you do this so that I may spend the rest of my life with companions who are like me."

Once more Olorun was pleased to do what Obatala asked. The sky god breathed life into the clay figures, which became living human beings. As soon as the figures were endowed with life, they saw Obatala's hut, and they began to build homes for themselves all around it. Thus was the first Yoruba village created. That village was called Ife, and it still exists today.

Obatala was very pleased with his work. Then, as the effects of the palm wine wore off, he saw that some of the people whom he had created were not perfect, and he promised that he would never drink palm wine again and that he would devote himself to protecting those who suffered because of his drunkenness. This is how Obatala became the protector of those who are born deformed.

The people whom Obatala had created needed food, so they began to work the earth. Since iron did not yet exist, Obatala presented his people with a copper knife and a wooden hoe, which they used to raise grain and yams. Ife slowly turned from a village into a city as the people prospered.

Seeing that his work on earth was done and having grown tired of being the ruler of Ife, Obatala climbed back up the golden chain to the sky. From that time afterward, he spent half of his time in the sky and half of his time in Ife.

When he was living in his home in the sky, Obatala told all of the other gods about the things that he had created on earth. Many of the gods were excited by his tales, and they decided to travel to the earth to live among the clay figures called human beings that Obatala had created. Before they left the sky, however, Olorun called them together and said, "Because you are gods, you must remember that you have certain obligations to the human beings. Among other things, you must listen to their prayers and help them when they need help." To each of the gods Olorun assigned a specific task that he or she would be responsible to fulfill on the earth.

Unfortunately, when he created the Yoruba world, Obatala had not consulted with Olokun, the ruler of the sea, and she became quite angry. She felt that he, a sky god, had usurped her power by changing a large portion of her domain and by assuming rulership over that kingdom. She thought long and hard, and finally she decided upon a plan that she felt would bring her revenge for Obatala's insulting actions.

One day, after Obatala had returned to the sky, Olokun brought together the great waves of her ocean world and flung them one after another across the land that Obatala had created. Before long the land was completely flooded and only marshland remained. The palm trees that Obatala had grown, the yams that the people had planted, and even most of the people themselves were washed away from the soil and drowned. The people who still lived called out to Obatala for help, but the noise of the waves was so great that he could not hear them.

The people found Eshu, the messenger god who had come to live among them, and asked him to carry their plea for help to Obatala and Olorun. Eshu told them to prepare a sacrifice to go along with their message in order to make sure that the great sky gods would listen to their plea, and he asked for a sacrifice for himself in return for his service. The people sacrificed a goat to Obatala and a white chicken to Eshu, and Eshu climbed back up the golden chain to tell Obatala about the flood.

Obatala was overwhelmed when he heard about the floods. He did not know how to deal with Olokun. Orunmila, after hearing about the destruction that the waves had brought to the land that Obatala had created, said that he would make the water withdraw. Orunmila climbed down the golden chain and used his vast power to make the waves return to the water. The marshland dried and the people pled with Orunmila to stay with them and protect them from Olokun. While Orunmila had no desire to remain in the Yoruba world, he agreed to teach both the gods and the humans who lived there how to foretell the future and how to control the forces that they could not see. Then he climbed back up to his home in the sky, though like Obatala before him, he felt a kinship with the Yoruba people and he often returns to their world to see how they are doing.

Olokun was not defeated yet, however. She decided to make another attempt to show that she was the equal of the ruler of the sky. A skilled weaver and dyer of cloth, Olokun challenged Olorun to a weaving contest.

Olorun knew that Olokun was the best weaver ever, yet he knew that he could not avoid her challenge, so he determined to accept it without actually undergoing the test. He called Chameleon and ordered him to go to Olokun with his reply: "Olorun, the ruler of the sky, greets Olokun, the ruler of the sea. Olorun asks that Olokun show his messenger, Chameleon, samples of the cloth that she has woven so that Chameleon can judge her skill. If Chameleon determines that the cloth that Olokun has woven is as beautiful as she claims, then Olorun will gladly engage in the contest."

Chameleon traveled down the golden chain to Olokun's abode, where he delivered Olorun's message. Olokun was pleased by Olorun's reply, and she put on a bright green skirt made from material that she had woven and dyed; amazingly, Chameleon turned the same color as the skirt. Olokun then put on a bright orange skirt; amazingly, again, Chameleon changed to the color of the garment. Next Olokun put on a bright red skirt; once more, Chameleon became the color of the skirt. For the rest of the day, Olokun put on the brightly colored skirts that she had woven. Each time Chameleon turned into the exact color of the skirt that she was wearing. By the end of the day, Olokun was ready to give up. She thought to herself that if even Olorun's messenger could duplicate the bright colors of her finest fabrics, surely the greatest of the gods could easily beat her in the contest. Therefore, she told Chameleon,

"Tell Olorun, your master and the ruler of the sky, that Olokun, the ruler of the sea, sends her greetings. Tell him that I acknowledge his superiority in all things, including weaving." Thus it was that peace was restored between Olorun, the ruler of the sky, and Olokun, the ruler of the sea, and that order again returned to the universe.

Nana Miriam

*T*he Songhai tribe lives along the
River Niger in Nigeria. In "Nana Miriam" a daughter
proves that her magical power is stronger even than that of
her father, and through this power she saves her people from
a terrible fate.

Nana Miriam

*I*n a village by the River Niger there lived a man named Fara Maka. Fara Maka was a large man, taller and stronger than anyone else in his village, but he was also a very ugly man. Ironically, Fara Maka had a daughter who was as beautiful as he was ugly. This daughter's name was Nana Miriam, and she was tall and strong like her father.

Fara Maka instructed his daughter about a great many things. For example, he taught her not only the names of all of the different kinds of fish, but also how to tell whether a fish was male or female. Over the years, Nana Miriam learned a great deal. In addition, she possessed magical powers that no one knew about. By using these powers, along with the magic spells that her father taught her, she became more powerful than anyone else in Songhai land.

Near the village of Fara Maka and Nana Miriam, alongside the River Niger, there lived a monster in the form of a hippopotamus. This monster was so insatiable that when it invaded the rice fields, it devoured the entire crop. These rampages soon brought famine to the Songhai. Unfortunately, none of the Songhai people could defeat this hippopotamus because it could change its shape at will. Many times the village's hunters spent long, weary days hunting for the monster, only to return in the evening unsuccessful, tired, and full of despair. As the famine grew worse, many people died.

One day, Fara Maka decided to try to kill the monster with his spear. However, when he came upon the beast, he grew afraid, for large pots of fire were hung around its neck. Fara Maka threw all of his spears at the horrendous hippopotamus, but each time the spear was destroyed by the fires. The animal simply turned its back on Fara Maka and went about its business.

Fara Maka became exceedingly angry. Because it was clear that he could not defeat the terrifying beast by himself, he turned to a member of the Tomma tribe who had a reputation as a great hunter. The hunter's name was Kara-Digi-Mao-Fosi-Fasi. Fara Maka went to this great hunter and asked if he would be willing to hunt the hippopotamus. Kara-Digi-Mao-Fosi-Fasi agreed to do so, and Fara Maka invited him and his hunting dogs, all 120 of them, to a great banquet in preparation for the hunt. Each dog, which had an iron chain around its neck, devoured the mound of rice and meat it was served, down to the last grain of rice. The hunter did likewise. Then the man and his dogs set out to find the monster.

Soon the hunting party came upon the huge hippopotamus, and the dogs were turned loose one by one. As each dog attacked the hippopotamus, the monster grabbed it and swallowed it whole. Kara-Digi-Mao-Fosi-Fasi ran away in terror, and the hippopotamus turned and walked into the nearest rice field, where it leisurely consumed all of the grain.

When the hunter returned to Fara Maka's home, he told the Songhai man and his daughter what had happened. When she heard of the destruction of the dogs and the rice field and saw the great hunter's terror, Nana Miriam stood up. "I think that it is time for me to see what can be done about this horrendous beast," she said.

Despite her father's qualms, she set out on her quest. It was not long before she came upon the hippopotamus devouring another rice field near the banks of the Niger. When the hippopotamus saw Nana Miriam coming, it stopped eating and said, "Good morning."

"Good morning," replied Nana Miriam.

"I think I know why you are here," said the monster. "You wish to kill me." He smiled and shook his head. "You must know, though, that no one can kill me. All the hunters of your village have tried; your father tried; Kara-Digi-Mao-Fosi-Fasi tried. They all failed. It is presumptuous for you, a mere girl, to think you can defeat me, when so many others of great renown have been unable to do so."

Nana Miriam replied, "We will never know whether I can defeat you until we have engaged in battle. I am ready if you are."

"Aha! Let the contest begin," shouted the hippopotamus. The very breath of the terrifying beast set the rice field on fire. A wall of flames through which no mortal could pass stood between Nana Miriam and the animal. Nana Miriam drew a magic powder from her juju bag[1] and cast it into the fire, whereupon the flames were turned into water.

"Excellent!" shouted the hippopotamus. Immediately an iron wall appeared between Nana Miriam and the hippopotamus. Nana Miriam reached into the air and pulled out a magic hammer. Using this hammer, she made short work of the iron wall, which broke into small pieces with the force of her blows.

For the first time, the monster was worried. Seeking to escape from this powerful girl, it turned itself into a river and tried to flow into the Niger. Nana Miriam pulled out another magic powder from her bag. The river dried up before it could reach the Niger, and the flowing water changed back into the giant hippopotamus.

Fara Maka happened along at this point looking for his daughter. The monster, now completely terrified, charged at Fara Maka. As it ran by Nana Miriam and was only ten yards away from her father, the girl seized its rear leg. With her great strength, she picked it up, twirled it around her head, and threw it across the river, where it smashed into some rocks on the opposite shore. The skull of the hippopotamus broke open, and the monster died.

Fara Maka was overjoyed. Having seen the mighty toss that defeated the monster hippopotamus, he could only exclaim, "What a magnificent daughter I have!"

When the father and daughter returned to the village, the whole tribe learned what had happened. From that time on, no Songhai starved because of the rampaging hippopotamus that used to devastate their rice fields, and from that day on the minstrels have sung the song of Nana Miriam's exploits.

---

1. *Juju bag,* a bag of charms.

The City Where People Are Mended

*T*he Hausa, who live in north-
ern Nigeria, are one of the three major tribal groups in the
country. Their language is used in much of Africa by traders. "The City Where People Are Mended" is a quest tale in
which two mothers undergo the same test but with very different outcomes.

The City Where People Are Mended

One morning all of the girls in the village went into the forest to pick herbs. They had no sooner gotten there than it began to rain and they quickly ran to a baobab tree and climbed into a hollow in its wide trunk.[1] While the girls were in the tree, the devil caused the hollow to close over. In order to release them, the devil said that each girl must give him her necklace and cloth. All of the girls but one gave the devil her necklace and cloth. The one who refused to do this remained enclosed in the hollow when the others ran back to the village.

On arriving at the village, the girls told the mother of the girl who had been left in the tree what had happened. Knowing that the tree had a small hole near the top, the mother prepared the evening meal and took it to the tree where her daughter was captive. She called out to the girl, "Daughter, daughter, stretch out your hand and take this food." The daughter did as she was instructed, and she took the food from her mother and ate it. After she was finished, her mother returned home.

A hyena, who had been hunting for game in the nearby bush, heard the mother talk to the girl and saw the girl take the food. When the mother left, the hyena went to the tree and called out, "Daughter, daughter, stretch out your hand and take this food."

The daughter was not fooled. "That does not sound like my mother's voice," she said, and she would not stretch out her hand.

Frustrated, the hungry hyena went to a blacksmith and asked him to alter his voice to make it sound like that of a human being. The black-

---

1. A baobab is an African tree with a trunk that can grow to thirty feet in diameter. Its fruit, which is called monkey bread, is edible, its leaves are used for medicines and spices, and its bark (which is sometimes used for medicine) is also used to make rope, cloth, and paper. Sometimes the trunk of the tree is hollowed out, and the Hausa believe that baobab trees house spirits.

smith agreed to do so, but he warned the hyena that if it found any food along the way, it should not eat the food before returning to the tree.

As the blacksmith had foretold, while the hyena was returning to the baobab tree he saw a centipede, which he ate. "After all, does one ignore food when it is found?" he said. He then finished his trip to the tree, where he called out, "Daughter, daughter, stretch out your hand and take this food." However, eating the centipede had affected the sound of the hyena's voice. Again the girl replied, "That does not sound like my mother's voice." Once more she refused to stretch out her hand.

The hyena returned to the blacksmith's shop very angry about what had happened. "My voice does not sound like a human's," he said. "Therefore, I am going to eat you." The blacksmith insisted that if the hyena did not eat him, he would make the hyena's voice sound like a human voice.

For a second time the hyena traveled back to the baobab tree. When he got there, he called out, "Daughter, daughter, stretch out your hand and take this food." This time the hyena's voice sounded like that of a human, and the girl stretched out her hand. When she did so, the hyena seized it in his strong jaws and pulled the girl out of the tree. For his meal he ate the girl entirely, leaving only the bones.

That evening when the girl's mother brought food for her daughter, she saw the bones lying on the ground and realized what had happened. She gathered up the bones, put them in her basket, and began walking to the city where people are mended.

After some time the mother came to a place where food was cooking itself. "Oh food, where is the road to the city where people are mended?" she asked.

The food answered, "Why worry about traveling such a long distance? Just stay here and eat me."

The mother replied, "I am not hungry, and I do not wish to eat you."

To this answer the food said, "After you have traveled awhile, you will come to two roads. Take the road on the side of the hand with which you eat and ignore the road on the other side."

The mother returned to her journey, and soon she came to some meat that was cooking itself. "Oh meat, where is the road to the city where people are mended?" she asked.

The meat answered, "Why worry about traveling such a long distance? Just stay here and eat me."

The mother replied, "I am not hungry, and I do not wish to eat you."

To this answer the meat said, "After you have traveled awhile, you will come to two roads. Take the road on the side of the hand with which you eat and ignore the road on the other side."

The mother returned to her journey once more, and soon she came to a *fura* that was mixing itself in a pot.[2] "Oh *fura*, where is the road to the city where people are mended?" she asked.

The *fura* answered, "Why worry about traveling such a long distance? Just stay here and eat me."

The mother replied, "I am not hungry, and I do not wish to eat you."

To this answer the *fura* said, "After you have traveled awhile, you will come to two roads. Take the road on the side of the hand with which you eat and ignore the road on the other side."

Leaving the *fura*, the mother continued her journey until she finally arrived at the city where people are mended. When she got there the people asked why she had come. "The hyena has eaten my child," she said.

2. When traveling some distance, the Hausa frequently carry bags of dry flour that they mix with water to make an edible paste, or *fura*. Mixed with sour milk, the *fura* is also used as a drink.

"Did you bring her bones with you?" the people asked. When the mother showed them the basket with her daughter's bones in it, they said, "Tomorrow we will mend your daughter."

The next morning, the people of the city asked the mother to tend to their cattle. The mother took the cattle from their enclosure and herded them into the fields to feed. The only food that was available for the cattle was the fruit of the *adduwa* tree.[3] The mother picked the fruits of the tree and gave the ripe ones to the cattle, saving the green ones for her own food. All day she gathered the fruits and fed them to the cattle until it was time to return to the city in the evening. When she returned home with the cattle, the largest bull of the herd cried out, "This mother has a good heart; mend her daughter well."

The people of the city, therefore, mended the daughter well, and the next day the mother and daughter returned to their home.

When they got back to their village, the mother's rival wife, who also had a daughter, was jealous because her own daughter was very ugly. Thinking that she might improve her daughter's looks, she devised a plan whereby she would kill her daughter and then go to the city where people are mended, as her rival had done.

The rival wife put her daughter in a pestle and pounded her to death. Then she took out her daughter's bones, put them in a basket, and headed down the road to the city where people are mended.

After she had traveled awhile, she came to the place where the food was cooking itself. "Oh food, where is the road to the city where people are mended?" she asked.

The food answered, "Why worry about traveling such a long distance? Just stay here and eat me."

The wicked mother replied, "You do not have to invite me to eat you twice," and she quickly ate the food.

---

3. The *adduwa* tree, also called the desert bait tree, is a thorn tree from which a gummy resin is collected.

She then continued on until she came to the place where the meat was cooking itself. "Oh meat, where is the road to the city where people are mended?" she asked.

The meat answered, "Why worry about traveling such a long distance? Just stay here and eat me."

The wicked mother replied, "You do not have to invite me to eat you twice," and she quickly consumed the meat.

Continuing on her journey, she came to the *fura* that was mixing itself in a pot. "Oh *fura,* where is the road to the city where people are mended?" she asked.

The *fura* answered, "Why worry about traveling such a long distance? Just stay here and eat me."

The wicked mother replied, "You do not have to invite me to eat you twice," and she quickly ate the *fura.*

On she traveled until finally she came to the city where people are mended. When she got there, the people asked why she had come. "My daughter is dead, and I wish that she be mended," she said.

"Did you bring her bones with you?" the people asked. When the mother showed them the basket with her daughter's bones in it, they said, "Tomorrow we will mend your daughter."

The next morning, the people of the city asked the mother to tend to their cattle. The mother took the cattle from their enclosure and herded them into the fields to feed. As she gathered the fruit of the *adduwa* tree, she set aside all of the ripe pieces, which she ate, giving the cattle only the green fruit to eat. When she returned home with the cattle, the largest bull of the herd cried out, "This mother has a bad heart; mend her daughter ill."

When the mended daughter was brought to her mother, the daughter had only been mended halfway. She had half a nose, one ear, one leg, one hand, and so forth. When she saw her daughter, the distraught mother said, "I am not your mother," and she ran away and hid.

The daughter followed her footprints until she found her mother. "Why do you run from me, mother?" she asked.

"Go away. You are not my daughter."

"No, it is you who say that you are not my mother, and it is true that it was someone else who brought me back to life. But you are the one who gave birth to me, and you are the one who is responsible for my misshapen body."

The horrified mother ran off again and she ran until she came to her hut. She hurried in and closed the door behind her. When the daughter arrived at the hut, she called out, "Mother, I am home." When the mother did not answer her, the daughter opened the door and went in to her mother. The rival mother and her hideous daughter lived the rest of their lives together. For as long as they lived, the wicked mother was haunted by the fact that her own daughter was so ugly while the daughter of her rival was so beautiful.

The King Who Was a Servant

*T*he Wolof people live in what is now known as Senegal. In "The King Who Was a Servant," a king is made to see his relationship to his people more clearly.

The King Who Was a Servant

*A*t one time a great king named Sabar lived in the town of Sedo. The king's armies were so powerful that they conquered many nearby towns and villages, and as a result many people had to pay tribute to Sabar. Indeed, if the chief from a neighboring chiefdom came to Sedo, it was a wise thing for him to go to Sabar's house, kneel down, touch his forehead to the earth, and give valuable gifts to this powerful ruler.

As Sabar grew older he also grew prideful. After all, his word was law in his kingdom. And, in fact, it was the law in other places as well. Thus, he often said to himself, "I am the greatest of the great, and no one can contradict me. There is no one who is more powerful than I."

One day a minstrel passed through Sedo. When he heard of the minstrel's presence, the king ordered that the man be brought before him to provide entertainment. The minstrel sang a praise song and danced a praise dance to Sabar and all of his ancestors. Then he played the harp and sang this song:

> The dog is great among dogs,
> Yet he serves man.
> The woman is great among women,
> Yet she waits upon her children.
> The hunter is great among hunters,
> Yet he serves the village.
> Minstrels are great among minstrels,
> Yet they sing for the king and his slaves.

When the minstrel had finished his song, the king asked him what it meant. Answered the minstrel, "It means that all people serve, no matter what their status."

Sabar shook his head. "No, minstrel. Not all people serve. I, the king of Sedo, do not serve others—they serve me. Is this true or not?"

"I am but a poor, foolish minstrel," the other man replied. "Who am I to say that the king of Sedo does not speak the truth?"

While Sabar and the minstrel were talking, a wandering holy man came upon the scene. He asked them for some food. The minstrel said, "Great King Sabar, please permit me to share with this holy man some of the food that you have not eaten."

The king replied, "You have my permission. Just hurry up so that we can finish our talk."

"Thank you, Your Highness," said the minstrel. Then he took his harp and handed it to the king. "Please hold my harp while I get the food." The minstrel took some of the king's food and gave it to the holy man. Once again the minstrel turned to the king. "Now, great king," he said, "you have said what I was not able to say, for no one can contradict a king. First, you said that you do not serve others but that others serve you. Still, just now you have given a holy man some of your very own food, and you have held the harp of a poor, foolish minstrel while he served another. So, how can it be said that the king does not serve? Remember the wise counselors' proverb, 'The head and the body must serve each other.'"

Saying this, the minstrel retrieved his harp and finished his song:

> The soldier is great among soldiers,
> Yet he serves the clan.
> The king is great among kings,
> Yet he serves his people.

Three Very Fast Men

*E*xaggeration is often a com-
ponent of humor, especially in tales that come out of an
oral tradition. Among the Mende of Sierra Leone, the
story of the "Three Very Fast Men" contains several
examples of exaggeration.

Three Very Fast Men

One day three very fast young men left their village to go to their millet fields to begin their harvest. Shortly after they began to harvest the grain, it began to rain. The first man was carrying a basket of millet on his head, and because the ground was wet from the rain, he slipped. In fact, he slid from Bamako Town to Kati Town. As he slid, the basket of millet began to fall. As he slid past a house in Kati Town, the man reached through the window and grabbed a knife. He then cut the tall grass growing along the path, wove it into a mat, and placed it underneath him—all as he was sliding along. The millet fell from the basket onto the mat. Finally, the man stopped, poured the millet from the mat back into his basket, and said, "It is lucky that I was quick enough to be able to make a mat or I would have lost my grain."

The second man had a flock of forty chickens. When he went to harvest his millet field, he carried the chickens with him in baskets so that they could feed on some of the grain. As he was about to begin the harvest, a hawk plummeted out of the sky ready to seize some of the chickens in its talons. The man stopped his harvesting, ran to his chickens, picked them up, put them in the baskets, covered them, and then caught the plunging hawk by its talons. "What do you think you are trying to do?" he said to the hawk. "Are you trying to steal my chickens? It is a good thing that I am too fast for you."

The third young man and the first young man then went on a hunt. The first man saw an antelope and shot an arrow at it. The third man leapt forward at that very moment, caught the antelope, killed it, skinned it, pegged the skin in the sun to dry,[1] and finally cut the meat and placed it in his knapsack. Then he reached out and caught the first man's arrow as it arrived where the antelope had stood. Laughing, he said, "What do you think you are doing with this arrow? Are you trying to shoot my knapsack?"

---

1. To keep an animal skin from shrinking as it dries, the hide is stretched and wooden pegs are driven through it near the edges to keep it in place.

The Magical Mirror, Sandals, and Calabash

T O G O

*I*n Togo the story of "The Magical Mirror, Sandals, and Calabash" is told. It is a riddle tale, meant to elicit among the audience members a discussion of which of three sons performs best with certain wondrous powers that they have obtained.

The Magical Mirror, Sandals, and Calabash

*O*ne day when an old man's three sons were all grown, he called the three young men together.

"As you can see," he said to them, "I am growing very old. Soon I will no longer be able to provide for myself, let alone for all of us."

The brothers looked at their father and then at each other. They nodded in agreement.

The old man continued, "The time has come for you to go out into the world to see if you can provide for yourselves and perhaps for me in my old age."

Again the three brothers agreed. The very next morning they set out on their journey. After a while they came to a large river.

Once they had crossed the river, the eldest brother spoke to the two younger men. "I think that it is time that we go our separate ways," he told them. He then instructed his youngest brother to go to the left. His other brother he told to go to the right. He himself would go straight ahead. "In one year's time," he directed his brothers, "we shall all come back to meet again at this exact spot."

The brothers parted, each to go his own way. At the end of the year they all met again at the same place on the bank of the river. "What did you bring back from your travels?" the older brother asked the youngest.

"The only thing of true value that I found," replied the youngest brother, "was a mirror. It is a wondrous mirror. Whoever looks into this mirror can see every place in the world, no matter how far away it is."

Next, the oldest asked his other brother what he had found.

"I, too, have found only one thing of value," answered the second brother. "I have found a pair of sandals. They are a wondrous pair of sandals. Whosoever puts one on can walk to any place in the world with only one step."

"I also have found but one thing of true value," said the oldest brother. "The thing that I found is a small calabash filled with medicines."

At this point the brothers decided to look into the mirror to see how their father was doing. The youngest brother took out the mirror, and they all looked into it. The three brothers became very sad, for they saw that their father had died while they were gone, and he had already been buried. "We must return home immediately to see if there is anything that we can do," said the oldest brother. Without a moment's hesitation, the second brother pulled out the pair of magical sandals. Together the three brothers put their feet into the sandals, and in one step they were beside their father's grave. Now the oldest brother took out his small calabash filled with medicine. He poured the medicine on the grave. No sooner had the medicine landed on the grave than their father rose up revived and well. He greeted them happily.

Which of the three brothers was the best provider?

Afterword

*H*istory makes it difficult to limit the concept of West Africa to fifteen nations. Over the centuries there have been innumerable kingdoms and empires throughout this area, most of which no longer exist even if the descendants of the political entities do—the Sudanic states that spanned fifteen centuries, for example. Among these was Ghana in the fourth century A.D., and nine hundred years later there was the Mandingo state of Kangaba (known subsequently as Mali), plus the Songhai empire; the sixteenth-century city-state of Goa; non-Sudanic Kanem-Bornu; Kono; Benin (a nation that at its zenith may have eclipsed all other nations in this part of Africa); and the Yoruba, Hausa, Mossi, Akan, and Wolof states.

With the coming of the Europeans, the map became in some ways even more complicated, for political boundaries originally determined by language, religion, and bloodlines were indiscriminately ignored and new nations and borders were created with pens and paper. In some instances unrelated peoples were included in a common geographical unit (such as happened in Nigeria); in other cases, peoples of similar backgrounds (the Wolof of Senegal and Guinea-Bissau) were separated politically whether or not there was any real division in terms of their personal relationships.

In the case of Nigeria the British colonial ruler, Governor General Lord Lugard (Frederick Dealtry Lugard), arbitrarily defined the nation in 1914. His determination did not consider the fact that three quite distinct and incongruous cultures—the Hausa in the north, the Ibo in the middle, and the Yoruba in the south—were contained within the physical boundaries that he set by decree. The result of Lugard's decision to include all of these peoples under one flag has led to a century of civil war spawned by the lack of a common language, different religious beliefs (Islamic, animistic or tribal, and Christian), differing cultural values, and disparate economic systems.

Names for countries change at times even when boundaries do not—Liberia was known as the Pepper Coast and part of Nigeria was called the Slave Coast; the Gold Coast and Ghana are designations for essentially the same land, as are the Ivory Coast and Côte d'Ivoire. The distinctions become increasingly confused when one realizes that even maps drawn in the middle of the twentieth century are no longer accurate. The Pepper Coast, the Slave Coast, and the Belgian Congo no longer exist; Portuguese Guinea is now Guinea-Bissau; French Guinea is Guinea; Spanish Guinea has become Equatorial Guinea; French West Africa has become Mali; Dahomey has become Benin; German Kamerun is Cameroon; and French Equatorial Africa has disappeared and been replaced by the Congo.

Because these countries cover such an incredible number of diverse tribes, cultures, languages, and political and religious divisions, I have chosen Liberia as a representative example of West Africa. Needless to say, Liberia, as would be any other nation that I might have chosen for this purpose, is simultaneously typical and atypical of the countries that comprise what we call "West Africa." Still, an understanding of Liberia itself will help provide a picture of what the countries of West Africa are like and at the same time create an identifiable context for all of the tales that are included in this anthology.

Bordered by the Atlantic Ocean, Liberia is situated just under "the great bulge" and just above the equator in the center of West Africa. Founded in 1822 by the American Colonization Society of Massachusetts, the country has a mixed population of the area's indigenous peoples (95 percent) and Americo-Liberians (5 percent). The latter are the descendants of many African nations who arrived as freed slaves from the United States and the Caribbean, especially during the period between 1820 and 1865. On July 26, 1847, Liberia became a republic with a constitution modeled on that of the United States. The country is the oldest republic on the African continent and the only Black African state never to have been under colonial rule. Slightly smaller than the state of Pennsylvania, Liberia has a population of approximately 2,540,000. In April 1980, a bloody coup led by Samuel Doe overthrew the government of President William Tolbert. Subsequently, Doe was deposed in a civil war that began in December 1989 and lasted through 1990. Unfortunately, despite the actions of a coalition of West African peacekeeping forces, late in the summer of 1992 hostilities resumed and were still under way in 1994.

The folktale in Liberia provides one of the few detailed sources for understanding the lives and beliefs of the people of a country in which the population of the nonofficial societies far outnumbers that of the officially proclaimed society. The culture represented in these tales is much richer and more resonant than that of the Americo-Liberian ruling class—it is older and it is indigenous, as opposed to being modeled after a foreign prototype. (Much of the Americo-Liberian culture is essentially transported American or European culture.) The religious breakdown of the population, which includes 70 percent who adhere to tribal beliefs (sometimes identified as animism) as opposed to the 10 percent who are Christians and the 20 percent who are Muslim, suggests the relative level of importance of these groups in Liberia's societal makeup. In spite of the terrible civil war that has been ravaging the country, the spirit of true nationalism that began to move in Liberia in the mid-1970s is still apparent, and the importance of native folklore is becoming increasingly recognized.[1]

As this movement continues, a body of literature is bound to emerge that is useful in supplying information about the majority of people who comprise the nation. Given the fragile and transitory nature of oral traditions, the recording of folktales is especially important and rewarding, and there have not been many attempts to do this in Liberian history. In fact, while a few of the former slaves

---

1. Nowadays, the use of the word "native" is sometimes considered insensitive. In this volume the term is used to mean "original, growing, or produced in a certain place or region; indigenous . . . of, belonging to, or characteristic of the original inhabitants of a particular place . . . one of the original inhabitants or lifelong residents of a place" (*American Heritage Dictionary,* Third Edition). This usage is not intended to offend but rather is accepted descriptive terminology.

who were returned to Africa carried with them a knowledge of written English, it was not until the nineteenth century that indigenous languages were replicated in an alphabetical form. The Vai alphabet was invented around the middle of that century, though unfortunately the letters devised were impractical for everyday use. More successful were the attempts of two missionaries who used alphabets that they created. George Crocker, a Baptist, translated a series of school texts and portions of the Bible into the Bassa language, and J. Leighton Wilson was responsible for reproducing the New Testament in Grebo.

Historically, most of the native wealth in Liberia has been centered in Monrovia and held by Americo-Liberians. Because the American Colonization Society, which was responsible for creating Liberia in the nineteenth century and transporting former slaves back to Africa, indiscriminately collected its charges from all over the American continent and the West Indies, those ex-slaves were originally from many different areas in Africa. Very few had ancestors who had come from what was to become Liberia and even fewer had been born there themselves. As a result, the ruling class in Liberia has tended to be racially mixed and English speaking. Most of the children of this group went abroad for their college education. Consequently, the students who attended the University of Liberia primarily belonged to the various aboriginal tribal groups which lived outside the Americo-Liberian's territory or were pushed out by the newcomers.[2]

Among the aboriginal Liberians there are sixteen important tribal languages and several miscellaneous dialects. In terms of population the two largest groups are the Kpelle (pronounced "pel-ee", 20 percent of the total population), residing in North-Central Liberia, and

2. As with the word "native," the use of the words "tribal" or "tribe" is sometimes considered insensitive. In this text the term "tribe" is used in reference to "a unit of social organization consisting of a number of families, clans, or other groups who share a common ancestry, culture, and leadership" (*American Heritage Dictionary*, Third Edition). This usage is not intended to offend; it is included because "tribe" is the identifier that the Liberians themselves used when I was in Liberia and is still in common use there and in other West African countries today.

the Bassa (16 percent, who live generally along the central coast and somewhat inland). Other tribes are the Gio (8 percent), Kru (8 percent), Grebo (8 percent), Mano (7 percent), Loma (5 percent), Gola (5 percent), and Vai (3 percent). While some of these languages and dialects are similar enough to be understood by members of neighboring tribes, most are quite distinct.

The Liberian folktales in this volume come from various tribal groups. The sources were as follows: Kpelle, four; Mano, four; Bassa, one; Gio, one; Loma, one; Kru, one; Glaro, one; Yawuahun, one; one from the island of Grenada; one from Nigeria; one from Belgium; one from Arabian folklore; five unidentified. It is interesting to note that the folklore of different nations of West Africa, especially that of Ghana, Guinea, the Ivory Coast, Liberia, Nigeria, and Sierra Leone, is similar. And, as former minister of education A. Doris Banks Henries observed in 1966, in Liberia "tribal literature does not differ to any great extent from one region to another." What differences there are tend to be in the characters used in the stories rather than in the essence of the stories themselves. Thus, in areas where one kind of animal is prevalent, that animal is preeminent in the regional tales, and in other locales where different animals predominate, those animals are featured. These subtle differences in the folktales of the various regions increase our enjoyment of the stories and enhance our understanding of the cultures of West Africa. What better way, then, to learn about the peoples of West Africa than through their folktales?

About the Author

$\mathcal{S}$teven H. Gale is the University Endowed Professor in the Humanities at Kentucky State University. He received his B.A. from Duke University, his M.A. from the University of California at Los Angeles, and his Ph.D. from the University of Southern California. He has also studied at San Diego City College, San Diego State University, the Massachusetts Institute of Technology, and Christ Church, Oxford University. Besides Kentucky State University, he has taught at Los Angeles Metropolitan College, the University of Southern California, UCLA, the University of Puerto Rico, the University of Florida, and Missouri Southern State College (where he was first head of the English Department and then director of the campus-wide Honors Program). Most importantly, he spent a year at the University of Liberia as a Fulbright Professor of English and American Literature and as special advisor to the Liberian Ministry of Education.

Among Professor Gale's many publications are studies of two novels by Nigerian novelist Chinua Achebe and several essays on Liberian literature and culture. He has been invited to speak on numerous occasions about African literatures and cultures, and he has taught university-level courses on those subjects as well.

Professor Gale has lived in seven states, Puerto Rico, and Liberia. His travels have taken him around the world—to forty-one states and more than fifty foreign countries.

His interest in West African folktales was stimulated by his experiences during the time that he lived in Monrovia, Liberia, and subsequently by his travels throughout Africa. In addition to his aesthetic appreciation of folktales, his scholarly publications and teaching about African literatures and cultures have helped him understand and appreciate the genre.